Supporting Learning in Primary Schools

Second edition

Supporting Learning in Primary Schools

Second edition

- **Rosemary Sage**
- **Min Wilkie**

Learning Matters

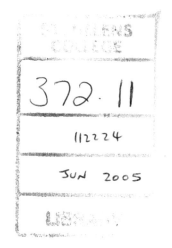

Every effort has been made to trace copyright holders and to obtain their permission for the use of copyright material. The authors and publisher will gladly receive any information enabling them to rectify any error or omission in subsequent editions.

First published in 2003 by Learning Matters Ltd.
Second edition published in 2004

British Library Cataloguing in Publication Data
A CIP record for this book is available from the British Library.

ISBN 1 844450 21 X

Project management by Deer Park Productions
Cover design by Code5 Design
Typeset by Pantek Arts Ltd, Maidstone, Kent
Printed and bound in Great Britain by Bell & Bain Ltd, Glasgow

Learning Matters Ltd
33 Southernhay East
Exeter EX1 1NX
Tel: 01392 215560
info@learningmatters.co.uk
www.learningmatters.co.uk

Contents

Introduction

This book has been written as a general guide to supporting teaching and helping children to learn for those working in support roles in primary schools. It will be useful to teaching assistants who are studying for higher education qualifications such as the Foundation Degree in Educational Studies or Learning Support, or Higher National Certificate/Diploma (HNC/D). In particular it addresses the needs of those training for Higher Level Teaching Assistant (HLTA) status; all the reflection points, tips and activities in this book have been cross referenced to the HLTA standards to facilitate the gathering of pertinent evidence. Cross references are in brackets (e.g. [1.2]) and the HLTA standards are set out in Appendix 1. It will also be useful to those following Specialist Teacher Assistant (STAA, STAC) courses, or NVQ3 and beyond, or for use during in-house training by teachers and mentors, as part of their training programmes. For teaching assistants not engaged in any sort of training, it is a handy resource to access for support as you go about your day-to-day work.

The role of the teaching assistant (TA) has developed and changed significantly over the last few years. It is widely acknowledged now that teaching assistants play a key role in children's learning and, as such, need the support of both informal and formal training to help them continue to develop professionally. We believe that support staff can, and should, maximise their potential to play a vital part in the school team and help to raise standards in schools.

The transformation in the role of teaching assistants is due in part to the emphasis that the Department for Education and Skills (DfES) is placing on the training of teaching assistants and the provision of a structure for career development. Whilst the responsibility for initiatives regarding pay and status remains with local education authorities (LEAs), the Government, through the DfES, has provided funding to employ greater numbers of teaching assistants and supported the development of training programmes to facilitate a better qualified and more informed workforce. You may find it useful to look at **www.teachernet.gov.uk//Professional_Development/managingmycpd/teach ingassistants/** and **www.hlta.gov.uk** for more information.

This book combines the underpinning theoretical knowledge and the practical classroom ideas to support teaching assistants in their exploration and development of skills and abilities to help them be effective and skilled in their role. Many people we have worked with, and spoken to, have expressed a desire for guidance regarding their personal study skills, so the final chapter includes some advice for those who have embarked on formal training already, or are about to do so.

The book covers the following five topics:

- the role of the teaching assistant;
- children's development;
- skills to support learning;
- organising effective learning;
- developing your own learning.

Throughout the book we have incorporated 'thumb-nail sketches' of real people in real roles to illustrate key points, as well as suggestions for activities that the teaching assistant, or trainer, can use as a basis for investigation (in the knowledge that, even though there will be points in common, each situation and each school is unique).

We hope that you will enjoy exploring your role and developing your knowledge of how schools work, and how children, teachers and schools can be best supported.

1. The role of the teaching assistant

Overview

This chapter is structured around the four strands of the role of a teaching assistant as identified in the Department for Education and Skills (DfES, 2000) publication *Working with Teaching Assistants: a good practice guide: support for the pupil, the teacher, the curriculum and the school*. It explores four key issues:

- who the teaching assistant (TA) might be within the primary school;
- how and why the role has developed;
- what part the TA might play within the school team;
- the significance of the contribution of the TA, including a view of possible future developments.

The incipient revolution

Whether you have been involved with schools for a long time or whether your interest is recent, you will be aware of some of the changes that have been happening, especially since the early 1990s, in the way that adults work in the classroom. The following stories will, perhaps, strike a familiar cord.

Ann's story

I trained as a nursery nurse, and got my NNEB, in 1987. I got a job in a nursery class for three to five-year-olds in an infant school. The teacher I was working with used to tell me what topic we would be working on that half term, and which weeks we'd be doing what, and I would plan daily activities to fit in. There were also the paints to do, the aprons to wash by hand weekly, the toilets and so on, though they had stopped washing the sand by then! A couple of years later I was working with a different teacher and we were much more a team – you wouldn't be able to tell straight away who was who if you came into the classroom. I used to take the story and singing sessions, and the school involved us in meetings and planning much more. Now I work alongside the SENCO with the infants, especially with special needs children. I monitor their IEPs, attend case conferences and write reports. I've done all the in-service training on literacy and numeracy and so on and been on quite a few other courses run by the LEA, as so much has changed since I trained. Now my children are older, I'm about to start on a part-time course. I think that, at 33, I've still got time to qualify as a teacher.

Paul's story

I am self-employed so that I can be flexible for my children, as my wife is a lawyer and works long hours. Being flexible time-wise was especially important as our son has dyspraxia. When he went to school I used to go in and help out a couple of times a week. I was really interested to see how small children learn, though the thought of a whole class of five-year-olds was a bit intimidating! I helped with reading, and took groups to work on the computer. I started taking groups to work on design technology projects. I enrolled on the STAA course, which was advertised for parent volunteers as well as classroom assistants, to find out more about what children are being taught. Its completion coincided with the start of ALS, and the head asked me if I'd like to take some groups starting that September. I've been doing it ever since, and I love it. Last year I took on the Starspell scheme as well – we're giving it a trial in Year 2. I really feel part of the school.

Whilst Paul is not typical, in that he is a man, and most TAs are white women aged between 31 and 50 and working part time (OU/Pricewaterhouse, 2001), neither of these stories is unusual. What is clear from these sketches is that the role of those whom we now call teaching assistants has been changing. This change was described in the same study as *an incipient quiet revolution*. It seems that much has happened but there has been little general awareness of the resulting developments, so let's think about some of those issues now.

REFLECTION POINT 1 [1.4]

- Talk with another TA about how you secured your job.
- Consider whether your attitude towards your role has changed since you began your employment.
- Think about what changes have made a difference to you during the time you have been working in your current school.
- Ask a teacher you work with what changes in the last five years have made a real impact on the way they work.

I wonder if your teacher mentioned support in the classroom? You might like to remember this response later in the chapter! Teachers are being asked to manage other adults in addition to teaching children, and while some could be better prepared, and most have had no training, the majority welcome as much support as possible.

What has driven this evolution from a fairly menial, or casual helping, role to one that is an essential part of the whole school team – a para-professional, or para-educational as employees in this role are known in the USA? Later in this chapter, we'll use the four strands of the role of a TA as identified in *Working With Teaching Assistants: a good practice guide*: *support for the pupil, the teacher, the curriculum and the school* (DfEE, 2000) to give structure to a detailed examination of issues relating to the way additional adults work in primary schools, and to help us to project into the future. Firstly, let us consider status in the light of 'the three Ns': names, numbers and knowledge.

The three Ns

What's in a name?

'Teaching assistant' is the currently preferred term to describe any support staff who work directly with children within schools. There are many different titles in use to describe roles that carry specific or general responsibilities, but the need was felt for a generic term that would encompass them all and reduce confusion (DfES, 2000). If you are not described as 'nursery nurse' or 'teaching assistant' you may be known as one of the following, which are all in common use across the country:

● classroom assistant;
● general assistant;
● learning support assistant;
● special needs assistant;
● specialist teacher assistant.

Sometimes these differences in title reflect the funding for particular posts, which may come from a variety of sources. For instance, you might be employed as part of a specific initiative, such as working within Reception classes, Education Action Zones, English as a Second Language, or as in Peterborough, through 'Enhanced Resource Provision' for children with communication difficulties. Until around 1998 in Leicester City, job descriptions only used the terms 'nursery nurse' or an 'ancillary', whatever the role. The proliferation of titles has been comparatively recent.

REFLECTION POINT 2 [1.4]

● Which titles are being used in your workplace?

● Do they denote differences in the responsibilities of the people involved?

● If there is a variation in titles, does this affect the day-to-day practice, or the way people are perceived?

Does a title, or name, matter? Well yes, it does. Estelle Morris, former Secretary of State for Education, held office while significant developments to the role of TAs took place. She said, *I see the school of the future as one where learning is supported by a range of well-trained staff, whether teachers, teaching assistants, or others* (Morris, 2002). Yet the co-author, Hancock, of a study by the Open University and Pricewaterhouse pointed out that *a lot of assistants, when they took on the work, didn't see it as a proper job...suddenly these women realised they were doing serious work* (Slater and Dean, 2001).

Words carry associations. Titles are the same. I know most of us can recall being amused at the re-naming of a job – what difference does it make if you are called a dustbin man or a refuse collector? Well, the second title implies respect for the service to the community. The noun 'ancillary', for instance, is defined in the Chambers English Dictionary (1993) as 'maid servant', and hopefully, though this might have been appropriate once, this is not how anyone would perceive the role in the twenty-first century. In 2001 the terms 'Mums' Army' and 'pig ignorant peasants' (Nigel de Gruchy will probably never bury that epithet), both derogatory, were used during debates regarding the role of TAs. The manner in which you are described affects the way people see you, treat you, and, most importantly, the way you think about yourself.

Working with children means that you probably already realise that it pays to be positive. Rosenthal and Jacobson (1968) showed that if children were labelled as 'naughty' or 'thick' then that is what they were likely to become. You might have heard of the 'self-fulfilling prophecy'. A study on under-achievement of children in schools showed that when teachers expected those children not to excel, that is exactly what happened. The results were indeed poor – probably because they were receiving the message, through the way they were addressed and the level at which their work was pitched, that they weren't as good as others and so began to believe it themselves. Promoting self-esteem leads to confidence in tackling situations and challenges. All those involved in education need to acknowledge, as Hancock (ibid) stated, that the role of the TA is indeed serious work.

Try filling in the table that follows [1.6]. In each column think of three more examples of actions that would show how you and your colleagues perceive the role of the TA. These may, or may not be a part of your actual experience. Some ideas have been given to start you off.

YOU		YOUR COLLEAGUES	
POSITIVE	NEGATIVE	POSITIVE	NEGATIVE
I have been asked to work with a child who has Aspergers syndrome so I looked it up on the internet.	I don't offer ideas as I'm there to carry out instructions.	My teacher gives me a plan, which includes me, at the beginning of the week.	I don't go in the staffroom at lunchtime as only teachers are allowed in there then.

Perceptions of the TA's role

Number-crunching

The number of people in support roles in schools has risen significantly:

> *Official figures show that the number of support staff in schools has already risen from 113,191 in 1997 to 157,181 last year (2001), with teaching assistants accounting for 34,000 of the 44,000 increase.*
>
> (Slater, 2002)

Official DfEE statistics for 1991 and 1994 gave figures of 13,641 and 21,914 respectively. It was calculated that in 1994 there was the equivalent of one full-time TA to eight teachers across primary schools (Moyles, 1997: 18). In your school you may now have more support staff than teachers and it seems it is the intention to continue this development, as the plan is to recruit a further 20,000 TAs between 2002 and 2006. This may be, in part, a response to the difficult situation that, *threatens to undermine Labour's education reforms* (Slater and Dean, 2001): the problem of teacher recruitment. It has been estimated that by 2006 there will be 40,000 unfilled teaching posts.

A related issue is the number of hours teachers work: appointing more TAs who could share some of the burden would be one way of addressing this problem. There are other reasons for this rapid growth (48 per cent increase in the number of TAs as compared to one per cent increase in teachers in the same period) but at least this strategy of recruitment shows that there is a general appreciation of the part TAs play in education and certainly raises their status.

This is reassuring, but most TAs will feel that the numbers issue that would really mark the arrival of the para-professional is that of remuneration. A Nursery nurse who is appointed as a nursery nurse, most commonly in Reception classes or in special schools, has a salary scale and a career ladder, but the majority of TAs work on temporary contracts for hourly pay which is often lower than the lunch-time supervisors or cleaners.

In 2002 some TAs faced potential salary *cuts*. The Professional Association of Teachers (PAT) – which has TA members, as do a number of other unions, including Unison and ATL – voiced concerns over new national terms for council workers that introduced a 37-hour working week, as opposed to the 32.5 hour full-time week worked previously. This would mean losses in real terms if people continued to work the same hours. More positively, however, systems of grading, which enable the recognition of qualifications, have been introduced: for example, Solihull introduced four salary bands in September 2001 and Nottingham brought in a three-band system shortly afterwards.

Gaining 'the knowledge'

Have you been on any courses lately? The chances are you have, since opportunities for the training of TAs have grown enormously over the last few years. Prior to the 1990s there was a clear distinction between nursery nurses, who completed a two-year course leading to, perhaps, an NNEB or a BTEC Diploma in Childhood Studies (remember Ann's story?) and others with little or no training in education. Even nursery nurses in schools had very little opportunity to attend courses. I remember the excitement of my nursery nurse colleagues in the late 1980s when they were offered a one-day course, the first for many years...in the summer holidays! Since then, short courses run by local education authorities (LEAs), the four-day induction training, Specialist Teacher Assistant courses and Foundation Degrees are just some of the training opportunities available to TAs.

REFLECTION POINT 3 [1.6]

- Ask two or three other TAs about courses that they've attended in the last year, and add these to a list of your own. Which opportunities are most commonly offered? Are these courses what they and you see as most useful?

- Consider keeping a log, or file, of the training you do in and out of school, as this will be useful to look back on in terms of your professional development when being appraised or applying for promotion or a new job. See Chapter 5 for tips on keeping a reflective journal.

These three issues – names, numbers and knowledge – are indicators that the UK is moving towards the professionalisation of TAs. Some LEAs do require a qualification of some kind before agreeing to employ a TA. For example, as mentioned above, Nottingham has decided to employ three grades of TA, each of which has specific benchmarks that include training, experience and responsibility. This move towards professional status mirrors what has been happening for several years in the USA, where about half the states now require certification for their 'para-professionals' to gain work in schools (**www.aft.org**).

The four areas of support

The four areas of TA support – for the pupil, the teacher, the curriculum and the school – interrelate, so you may find that some issues are covered in two or more of the following sections.

Support for the pupil

> **Claire's story**
>
> *Matthew has Downs syndrome. He's an energetic little boy, and he wants to be involved in everything. When it was time for him to start school, at four plus, a place was available for him in the local primary school with designated hours for support. I am a qualified nursery nurse, and I was already working as a teaching assistant in a nearby school when I saw the job advertised. I felt the school was particularly interested in me as I had just completed the Specialist Teacher Assistant Award as well as having the right experience for the role. I work alongside the teacher and the nursery nurse, and help Matthew to take part in everything the rest of his class does.*

Can you think of some advantages and disadvantages of integration for Matthew – one for each box? [2.8] [3.3.7]

	ADVANTAGES	DISADVANTAGES
Facilities/resources		
Achievement		
Self-esteem		

Would Matthew have had the opportunity to enjoy his local school if he had been born in the middle of the twentieth century? You'd be right if you thought not! Support for the pupil is not only about working with children with special needs: in fact, the shift in attitudes and provision for such children has been the root cause of the development of the role of the TA. If you look back to the discussion on numbers you will realise that the rise in numbers of TAs in school correlates closely to the inclusion of special needs children within mainstream provision. These children would often need support for social or medical reasons, for example, and so began the growth of assistants for special needs. Inclusion has to be dealt with sensitively. McNamara and Moreton (1993) point out that integrating children is not a simple matter. They cite a small-scale study by Lalkhen and Norwich (1990) which demonstrated that normality will not rub off on students: something has to be done to foster self-esteem and to enable integration to work.

Legislation on inclusion, and the resulting practices, has had an impact on the working conditions of TAs. Consider the summary of legislation that has affected inclusion in Appendix 2. It is important to appreciate the statutory frameworks within which we must work. For more information about Special Educational Needs and the Code of Practice see Chapter 4. You might have been given hours to support a particular child, as Claire was. Under this kind of contract, if the child left the school, the job disappeared. This job insecurity is experienced by many TAs who support individual pupils with special needs.

The level of contact that a TA has with children and the type of support they offer has changed immensely. In 1986, when I began my first job as a primary teacher in Leicestershire, there were only two ancillaries in the school. The head would not allow parent helpers or ancillaries to carry out any activities in the classroom. Parents helped maintain the library and made costumes for the school productions. Ancillaries could carry out craft activities in the art area outside the classroom, mix paints, photocopy, provide resources such as videos, but they were very definitely not allowed to encroach on the teacher's 'patch', which included hearing readers. However, when interviewing classroom assistants during their 1997 study, Moyles and Suschitzchy (p. 25) found that:

> many staff may have originally been employed to provide for the social aspects of children's needs in schools and, therefore, still perceive this as an important part of their role.

If we think back to the numbers issue mentioned earlier, and relate it to this study, we see that, because many more TAs were employed as a direct result of inclusion policies at a national level, so the remit for TAs changed, at least in part, to reflect the fact that many were employed specifically to support individual children. The same study also found that training was having an impact on the way TAs work with children. Knowing about the way children learn, for instance, helps a TA make choices about how to present work or what to expect (see Chapter 2 for more about this). Moyles and Suschitzky compared TAs with training (STAs) and those without training (CAs) and observed that *CAs frequently carry out some of the work for children and therefore do not encourage independence. The STA training may have emphasised the importance of independent learning* (ibid).

Children who become used to support, and expect others to do things for them are said to have acquired *learned helplessness* (Merry, 1998: 77). When Farrell et al (1999) discussed good practice of TAs (whom they referred to as Learning Support Assistants (LSAs)), they remarked that LSAs would have a detailed knowledge of the difficulties and impairments of particular children. They would be concerned for these children and their Individual Education Plans (IEPs), and it would be appropriate to give short, intensive periods of help outside the classroom. But children should, ideally, be taught within a group of others so that they can be given 'space and distance' to develop independent learning strategies as well as support when needed: *You should be aiming to be so effective in promoting the independence of the pupil that you work yourself out of a job!* (Fox, 1998: 13) .

Some of the ways TAs are supporting children in accessing education in 2002 show how very different the role has become. You may be asked to read for children during National Tests, or support them in using ICT (Information and Communication Technology) to respond to their lessons. You may encourage children to meet the targets on their IEPs or be asked to liaise with professionals from outside school, for instance the speech and language therapist.

REFLECTION POINT 4 [1.3] [3.1.3] [3.3.3] [3.3.4]

- Look back at the changes you listed in the first section. Were any of them directly to do with working with pupils? Perhaps you can add some now.

- Why not carry out an audit of your own practice in supporting your pupils?

- Consider how you:

  a) show interest in your pupil and what effect this has;
  b) model or demonstrate desired objectives for social skills or academic learning.

Support for the teacher

Nikki's story

I work in one of two Reception classes. There are four permanent staff; two teachers and two teaching assistants. We are a really good team, and the TAs are involved with the planning, the assessment and everything really. I do baseline assessment tests in September, and I work with groups of children during the literacy hour and daily maths lesson. We bounce ideas off each other. I think our relationship is great. Just after Christmas I was carrying out an ICT task for a course I'm doing. It involved scribing for a few of the children to enhance their story-telling skills and I was using the programme 2Simple, an Infant Toolbox. Cath, the teacher, was so impressed she asked if we could use the idea with the whole class, so they all retold the story behind a nursery rhyme, and then decorated the border using their own computer-generated pictures.

It is quite possible to look back to a decade ago, and remember when it was fairly common for extra adults in the classroom to be seen as an intrusion, or a threat to the teacher's autonomy. Attending to the needs of 31 four-year-olds without support would be unacceptable now...and it was a challenge then! I'm not suggesting this was a policy adhered to everywhere. Indeed I had been a parent volunteer in my children's open-plan school for cooking and library duties myself and been made very welcome (but not in the staffroom). A case study (Gold, 2001) illustrates how teachers' attitudes have developed. The Special Educational Needs Co-ordinator (SENCO) of Bay House School in Hampshire said:

> *We started taking statemented children and the special needs assistants came with them. I had to introduce them by saying, 'This is a legal requirement, these children need this provision, we have no choice'. Now the teaching staff's attitude is 'Why can't you give me more help?'*

For the most part, teachers and TAs work together successfully but there are two key concerns:

- the training of teachers to manage TAs effectively and efficiently;
- the possible erosion of the teacher's role, and the necessity for all to understand the distinction between the two.

Managing teaching assistants

Teachers should understand that a good assistant is a resource to be treasured and not be afraid to give the TA responsibility (O'Grady, 2001). Managing people is a skill for which many established teachers have not had training and have had to develop whilst 'on the job'. The study by Farrell et al (1999) confirms this and stresses that investment in developing the managing skills of teachers is essential if the work done by TAs is not to be marginalised. They recommend that teachers and TAs be encouraged to learn together. From 1998, student teachers have had to *...demonstrate that they are able to manage...the work of parents and other adults in the classroom* (DfES/TTA, 2002).

As you will know, if you have experience of working in a number of partnerships, each working relationship is unique, and is built on trust, and on the recognition and inter-play between the strengths that each person brings to the 'partnership', as Nikki's story shows. Then, as confidence and familiarity with styles of teaching and organisation increase, you take on more – remember Paul?

An education bill published in November 2001 sought to find ways to reduce the workload for teachers, but it began a debate on what duties it would be appropriate to delegate to TAs and what would not. Farrell et al (1999) had identified some issues. For instance, where there were reports to write for reviews they found that most of their interviewees accepted that these were the responsibility of the teacher, but that TAs or LSAs were involved in the process and contributed in writing or verbally, especially with in-depth views of the IEP. The interviewees also thought that teachers planned, whilst TAs implemented those plans, but in practice Farrell et al found that TAs were planning work, especially for small groups, and on intervention programmes. Since then, as part of the remodelling of the workforce in schools (which began in 2003 after a National Agreement was signed in January of that year), a list of 25 duties that could be undertaken by staff other than teachers was developed, and implemented from September 2003. Much information is now available to TAs and other school personnel from sources such as **www.teachernet.gov.uk** and **www.hlta.gov.uk**.

TAs are also commonly found to be involved in assessment of pupils – in fact involvement in this way is recommended as good practice by the DfES (DfES, 2000). Such involvement has become increasingly vital as testing pupils becomes more formalised, and national testing has become a legal requirement. I remember teaching a Year 2 class in the second year of National Tests (SATs): at that time, teachers were offered TAs to support us whilst testing, but they had to supervise the remainder of the class with set work while the teachers did the testing. TAs now studying on the Foundation Degree and the STA (Senior Teaching Assistant) course in Leicester have described how they very often carry out tests themselves, for instance the national reading tests. Day-to-day assessment through feedback to the teacher has also become far more valued, as the teacher is able to capitalise on input from the TA to plan future lessons most effectively.

Comparatively recently, advice regarding the deployment of support staff included them making the most of whole-class teaching sessions by taking the opportunity to carry out *organisational tasks* such as cutting paper (Moyles, 1992:142). This came from the perception that support staff were non-teaching and were wasting time by listening to such discussions. However, evidence from Farrell et al suggests that, quite apart from the risk of distracting pupils, there are several very good reasons why TAs should be present and included during whole-class teaching. They state that all TAs should have *a detailed engagement with the aims, content, strategies and intended outcomes for the lesson* (1999: 37) for two reasons:

- Firstly, they gain a full understanding of not only the aims and purposes of the lesson, but also the language and vocabulary used in explanations. This enables them to maximise effectiveness by re-phrasing or re-presenting tasks in later group sessions.
- Secondly, they can support children with limited attention span, or behavioural difficulties to stay on task by using low-key gestures, or encouragement to participate as fully as possible.

Other tasks considered suitable for delegating to TAs are invigilating during tests, taking the register, and more controversially, covering for teacher absences, or the provision of non-contact time for teachers. This is an area which will continue to be examined, especially by the unions:

> *CAs have been described as the teachers' life support system and their separate, but distinct role at the chalkface must be more highly recognised … in parallel with teachers, not as a replacement.*
>
> (Unison newsletter, 2001).

REFLECTION POINT 5 [1.4]

- Has your job 'grown', as the relationship between the teacher/s you work with has developed?

- If you work with more than one teacher can you compare those experiences and identify features of the relationships which make you feel valued, and part of an effective partnership?

- Are there any duties that you carry out which you think should not be part of your remit?

Support for the curriculum

The 1990s have been termed *the decade of primary education* by Robin Alexander, part of a three-man team which was commissioned to write a report on curriculum organisation and practice (Rose, Alexander and Woodhead, 1992). At the beginning of that decade it was common practice for the delivery of the curriculum to be through the 'integrated day'. This was where classes were organised into perhaps four to six groups who revolved around a range of activities throughout the day. The teacher planned through topics, often following the interest of the children, and giving scope for a creative and imaginative experience, though since there wasn't the continuity or accountability of today's system, there was also a risk that the educational experience might not be balanced.

REFLECTION POINT 6 [2.3]

- Topic work is still part of the curriculum for non-core subjects and in the Foundation Stage. Obtain a plan of a topic from either of these areas.
- Consider what advantages there might be in delivering material in this way, apart from motivation through interest.

HMI evidence at the time showed that quite significant numbers of children were receiving little or no teaching at all in some areas of the curriculum. Taking into account the low numbers of support staff available then, additional adults in the classroom were as likely to be parent volunteers as 'ancillaries', who were usually engaged in practical activities. They would enhance the curriculum on offer by taking groups of children for cooking, sewing and, as Paul did, for other creative pursuits, or by listening to readers.

The advent of the National Curriculum, in 1988, made teachers and schools far more accountable for their planning. Schemes of work showing that the school had addressed each subject, and planned how it would be taught in each year group, had to be in place. TAs began to be more involved in working with children within the classroom, and in supporting work that formed part of the core curriculum.

The National Literacy Strategy (NLS), which incorporated the literacy hour and was introduced in 1997, made a very great impact on the way classrooms operated. By the time the National Numeracy Strategy (NNS) was introduced there was no real place for an integrated-day approach. The exception was within Reception classes where children who were entitled to the National Curriculum were allowed to participate in a more relaxed delivery mode, with follow-up work from the whole-class teaching session being carried out at different times of the day. Both of these strategies stressed the importance of the presence of an additional adult, especially during the middle part of the lesson, where children were working individually or in groups. Suddenly TAs had to be working directly with children, and found themselves timetabled far more intensely, despite the fact that they were expected to continue with all the other tasks they had always done – hence the title *Jills of all Trades* (Moyles and Suchitzky, 1997). The latter study found that schools would rather appoint extra TAs to support this work, as they could afford more of them. It recognised through observations, that sometimes the value of input might not have been of an optimum level, as TAs without training did not always have the questioning skills or subject knowledge. Those with STA training were more effective, which led them to recommend an increase in opportunities for training.

The catch-up programmes, of which the Additional Literacy Strategy (ALS) introduced in 1999 was the first major national example, heralded a real development in terms of responsibility and practice for TAs. These programmes had been written with the expressed intention that they would be delivered almost entirely by support staff. Although the sessions were 'scripted', TAs were, essentially, teaching small groups. They had to prepare resources, keep progress notes and record, and as their confidence grew they began to plan adaptations.

REFLECTION POINT 7 [2.2]

- Are you involved with the whole curriculum, or do you work mostly within particular curriculum areas? What are the advantages and disadvantages, do you think, of both modes of deployment?

Support for the school

Meriel's story

I had been working in Key Stage 2 for some years. I was also a governor at the school, having got involved when my own children went there. They're grown up now. The changes in the curriculum and the way we worked had been quite significant. My colleague and I decided to try the STA course in order to feel better informed about the background to our everyday work. We became very interested in improving our service to the school and, while we were studying, we managed to negotiate team meetings for TAs which had never happened before. Over a period of time we have made several suggestions for adapting practice which have been adopted by the school, and made working together much better. The teachers have been interested in what we are doing and very supportive.

Working within the whole school team

All TAs, however described, are part of the whole school team, *...and as such their remit includes translating school policies and furthering the ethos of the school* (DfEE, 2000). There is a two-way transaction here – TAs need support in terms of good management and professional development to carry out their job effectively. Both the following sections relate to school improvement, and every school should now have a PANDA (Planning and Achievement Document), which includes details of staff development plans and proposals for meeting targets.

Whole school issues

Areas of school life that involve everyone include topics such as behaviour, special educational needs, health and safety and child protection. Ensuring that you adhere to and reflect the policies of your school or LEA on all such matters is a vital part of contributing to the success of the school.

One of the most valuable contributions to teamwork made by TAs is in working with children who have particular needs. These may be recognised Special Needs, though many children's needs stem from other causes, for instance emotional turmoil, such as bereavement or abuse. The discussion of strategies for working with children in later chapters of this book will serve to support the school, especially regarding behaviour. However, it is appropriate to consider some aspects of health and safety and child protection here.

After the stabbing of Philip Lawrence, the London Head Teacher, in 1995 and the horror of the shooting in Dunblane in 1996, school security and health and safety issues became key areas for the attention of school teams. Many schools have implemented so many security measures that having an open door policy for parents has been made extremely difficult. In a report commissioned by the Secretary of State (**www.dfes.gov.uk/schoolsecurity/wgssreport1.shtml**) the training of TAs in the area of health and safety was advocated as it was 'recognised that support staff were often in front line when it came to dealing with problems of security, safety and discipline'. TA involvement will be addressed in school policies on behaviour, and child protection in addition to health and safety. Keeping yourself safe as part of the team includes having an awareness of the policies regarding contact with children. Recently one TA reported that all staff at her school had been directed never to lift a child onto their knee. While this is a sad move, and contrary to the type of care many TAs give in the Early Years or in nurture groups, it is in some ways understandable. It is important to take care not to put yourself or any other team member in a vulnerable position. Not being alone with an upset parent, or with a child who needs personal care are just a couple of examples of ways of keeping health and safety secure.

If you work with groups, however, you are likely to develop relationships with children that have dynamics that are both different and complementary to the relationship teachers have with children. You become a 'bridge'; a supportive professional adult who is more closely involved with individuals. School policies normally advise that in the event of a disclosure TAs (and other adults) should never promise to keep a secret, or ask probing questions but should always let the child know they are taken seriously and will be helped. More information can be found at **www.teachernet.gov.uk/wholeschool**.

Conditions of employment and professional development

It is important to know how TAs fit into the school team. This will vary, depending on factors such as size which necessitate more departments. The line manager of a TA may be a class teacher, the SENCO, the head, or sometimes a teaching assistant appointed to a managerial position.

REFLECTION POINT 8 [1.4] [3.1.2] [3.3.8]

- Make a diagram like the one below to show the relationships between different staff, and how TAs fit into the team within your school.
- Consider how one of the issues to do with health and safety or child protection highlighted in the previous section is dealt with in your team.
  - Who is responsible/who is the designated member of staff?
  - How would you report an issue that had come to your notice?
  - Would any other agencies need to be involved?

Heritage Park Primary School – staff organisation

Effective communication between all members of the school team is of fundamental importance. This begins with knowing the expectations of the job. The DfES Good Practice Guide(2000) re-iterated the right for all employees to have a clear and accurate job description. The National Occupational Standards, published in 2001, and the guide mentioned above, both advise on the format and content of adequate job descriptions. However, at the time of writing, some TAs do not have a job description of any kind. Ideally, TAs should be involved with the drawing up and regular reviewing of their job descriptions.

REFLECTION POINT 9 [1.6]

- Use the example of the job description found in *Working with Teaching Assistants: a good practice guide* and compare it with your job description. If you haven't got one, write your own and compare it!

- Did you have an interview and/or an induction? If you had to carry out induction for a new colleague what would you include?

- Look through your school's PANDA. Are there any references to TAs?

Paul's story, which we met earlier in this chapter, is typical of how many TAs begin their jobs, but the way Claire was appointed is far more worthy of the growing professional status of the TA. Being appointed through an interview, which is followed by induction, and then a regular appraisal gives the message that this work is serious, a proper job with proper staff. Induction should address the location and contents of school policies. The introduction of inspections by OFSTED, and the necessity to demonstrate how schools have answered the challenge of accountability, has resulted in them developing policies to support and explain their practice. The ethos of the school will be explained through the school mission statement, to be found in the prospectus. This will also have shortened versions of policies that should be available to all staff. Being familiar with and upholding policies such as the behaviour policy, or the equal opportunities policy shows support for the school team.

TAs very often contribute to maintaining the ethos of the school by participating more widely in whole-school activities, for example by becoming a school governor or running extra-curricular activities at lunchtime or after school.

With a permanent contract, in addition to better terms, it is more likely that time can be built into the day to attend meetings and in-service training. Training is essential for all TAs, since better informed people will be more effective in their role with children, and thus both the children and the school will benefit. This has been acknowledged by OFSTED (1999) in DfES (2000: 7): *...well-trained teaching assistants are a key resource and are used very effectively in many primary schools.* It should be remembered that nursery nurses have professional status already.

Since the mid-90s, opportunities for training have become more diverse and more accessible. Now there is a range of courses from level 2 (GCSE equivalent) to degree level, short-term and extended, in colleges and universities, or in-school through NVQs. Flexible routes to suit everyone! The creation of a formal career structure offering opportunities for training, qualifications and career progression looks likely. The union PAT has proposed a 'Chartered Teaching Assistant' scheme (2000) to address this. From 2004 many TAs will have attained Higher Level Teacher Assistant

(HLTA) status, and their LEAs may have implemented a local career structure. Some TAs with additional responsibilities are being appointed to administrative roles, where they take on the responsibility of organising the timetables and professional development for the rest of their team. Others are acting as SENCO or sharing the role with a teacher. Some may be providing short-term teaching cover, although this is still a contentious issue.

Raising achievement

Since 1998... schools have experienced an unprecedented amount of reform to raise standards of pupil performance (DfEE, 2000: 7). Many of the strategies intended to do this have already been identified earlier in this chapter. However there have been several measures to record and report achievement so that it can be seen whether targets are being met. You have probably been part of an OFSTED inspection, and hopefully, it was a constructive, positive experience. You cannot fail to have been part of the assessment process, which is discussed in Chapter 4. Setting targets gives everyone something to aim for. Striving to help all children reach their potential, however, is bound to contribute to the overall success of the school, and that is essential to the role of the TA.

Summary

If you have taken the opportunity to reflect on points raised throughout this chapter, you will have:

- discovered much about how the role of the TA has changed and is continuing to change
- analysed your own position within the context of your work and should be able to suggest ideas for change or some professional targets for yourself.

2. Children's development in an inclusive society

Overview

Can you conjure up a picture of a young baby writhing away on the carpet, cooing and gurgling, with no control over his movements and the world around him? Imagine him five years later as he starts school, running and jumping, chatting to his friends and making constant observations about things around. In a short time a child's brain and body have matured, through the care and stimulation of adults who have looked after him, until he is ready to tackle formal learning. So what are the development issues and how do they affect support for children? Let's glimpse these physical, mental, emotional and social aspects and consider the issues surrounding their development in a formal inclusive education system.

Physical development

Physical development sets limits not only on what children can experience but also on what they can learn. In addition, physical growth and change have an important effect on self-image and relationships. The experiences and interactions of unusually small children, who develop slowly, may be different from those of bigger, faster growing peers, especially in adolescence. My tall son and his tiny friend had an acrimonious parting in their teens because of physical differences. I grew fast and was bigger than friends at age 14, feeling like an elephant alongside fairies! A child compares her own self-image with an ideal in her head. Actual physical characteristics may be less important than feelings about them. What are the aspects of growth that we need to consider?

Height and weight

Would you believe a baby is one-third of final height, but the head is enormously large in proportion to the body? By three, children are half their adult height. In adolescence, a growth spurt comes earlier for girls but lasts for a shorter time resulting in a lower average height than boys. Body parts grow at different rates. The hands and feet grow fastest, followed by arms and legs, with the trunk being the slowest, giving a gangly appearance and awkward feelings. When I was twelve years old, I held forth to my teacher about a hockey match, making a grand gesture to demonstrate shots down the wing. I hit her in the face and was astonished that my arm was long enough to almost knock her out!

Bones and muscles

At birth, bones are soft, and they harden at different rates. The hand and wrist are the first to stiffen to grasp and pick up objects. Muscles change enormously in length and thickness. During adolescence there is a sharp increase in muscle tissue, particularly in boys, accompanied by a decrease in fat. Between 13 and 17 years, a boy's strength doubles and male/female differences become marked.

This may be an important issue in the academic performance debate. At a time when boys, particularly, are preoccupied with physical growth and need exercise, they are being increasingly asked to concentrate on mental activities. This causes tension, as school demands do not follow nature.

Movement

A baby's ability to control muscles and move around is striking. Table 1 below shows approximate ages and stages from a survey of child development norms operating in the UK (Sage, 1990).

APPROXIMATE AGE WHEN SKILL APPEARS	MOTOR SKILL
1 month	Lifts chin while lying on stomach.
2 months	Lifts chest as well as chin.
4–6 months	Rolls over from lying position.
7 months	Picks up objects using the palm without thumb and finger.
8–9 months	Sits up easily. Stands by holding onto something and then independently.
12–15 months	Takes first steps.
13–15 months	Grasps objects with thumb and forefinger.
18 months	Walks well alone.
2 years	Walks up and down stairs with both feet on each step. Runs well.
30 months	Walks on tiptoe.
3 years	Rides a tricycle.
4 years	Walks down stairs, one foot at a time. Throws a ball overhand.
4–5 years	Hops on one foot.

Table 1 Approximate milestones in motor development

There is progression in co-ordination from large to small body muscles and movements. The timing varies from one child to another and the above table offers a rough guide only. Moving is directly linked to bone and muscle development. Until neck and trunk muscles have matured it is impossible to hold up the head or sit securely. Practice is vital to facilitate progress and, if children have limited opportunities, motor development will be slower (Brazelton et al, 1969). Studies by Gesell et al (1929) indicate that practice is only useful once a child is ready to perform a skill. Williams and Scott (1953) found poor, black infants in Washington, DC demonstrating faster growth than those from middle-class families because they were less restricted and their parents more permissive. The maturational process undoubtedly sets limits on the rate of physical growth and motor development, but this may also be delayed by the absence of appropriate experience and practice.

REFLECTION POINT 10 [2.2] [2.5]

● Using the above guide, consider the motor development of two children:

– What are the similarities and differences in their maturation?

– What is the impact on other development?

Brain development

Brain growth has been less considered than body because it is not so easily seen. The three main brain areas are illustrated below (Sage, 2000):

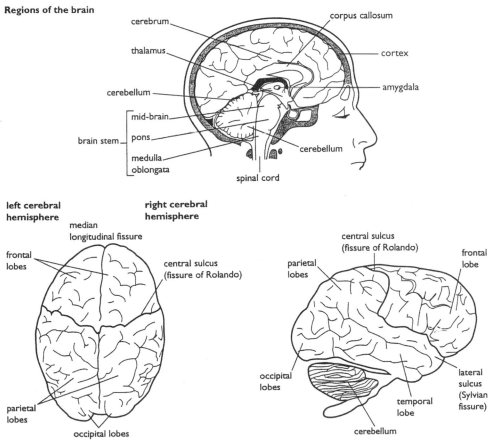

Regions of the brain (from Sage, R (2000) *Class Talk* published by Network Educational Press)

The approximate ages and stages of brain growth (from Sage, (2000) *Class Talk*) are set out below.

Conception–15 months: cerebellum development:

- survival systems: breathing, sleeping, waking, eating, elimination;
- sensory development: balance, hearing, touch, smell and seeing;
- motor development: reflexes integrate into movements of neck, arms and legs.

15 months–4.5 years: limbic system development:

- emotional exploration: feelings, emotions and their expression;
- social development: memory and relationships – self and others;
- large movement proficiency: walking, running, jumping, climbing.

4.5–7 years: global hemisphere development (usually right brain):

- sees whole picture: top-down processing: makes deductions;
- builds images from movement and feeling: rhythm, emotion, intuition;
- talks to develop thoughts: outer speech.

7–9 years: linear hemisphere development (usually left brain):

- processes detail: bottom-up processing: induces from details;
- develops complex language (clauses): understands sounds, letters, words in writing;
- uses logic/linear processing to solve problems; develops techniques.

8–9 years: frontal lobe development:

- fine motor proficiency: manual dexterity for writing and two-dimensional eye focus (fovea);
- internal language formed to regulate tasks and behaviour (inner language).

9–12 years: increased connections between right and left brain (corpus callosum):

- right and left brain integration;
- proficient top-down and bottom-up processing.

12–16 years: hormonal changes of puberty:

- body conscious: preoccupied with body functions of self and others;
- increases social and community interactions.

16–21 years: thinking skills extend:

- plans for future: considers ideas and possibilities;
- emotional and social maturity: independence and coping skills.

20–30 years: frontal lobes refine:

- formal reasoning: high level of thinking, reflection and insight;
- emotional refinement: altruism, love, understanding, compassion;
- fine motor skills: develops and sustains intricate manual activities.

30 years onwards: further refinements of physical and mental abilities:

- hands and face: greater finger and face agility for improved expressive powers;
- experience brings perspective, understanding and wisdom.

REFLECTION POINT 11[2.2] [2.5]

- What strikes you about this pattern?
- Can you find examples of educational practice that ignore brain growth periods?
- Reflect on brain growth in relation to school experience.

The cerebellum (hind brain)

The cerebellum includes the brain stem – pons, medulla and midbrain. It is the oldest, evolutionary part and develops from conception to 15 months. It monitors the outer world through the senses (eyes, ears, touch, sense of position in space, smell, taste) and activates the body to respond to survival needs. The Thomas and Chess study (1977) discovered adult competency stems from three factors:

- rich sensory experiences that build strong mental images;
- freedom to explore safely;
- adults who respond fully when children ask questions.

Hands-on sensory experience remains the basis for knowledge all through life, but active learning has reduced under National Curriculum demands. I observed a 12-year-old girl in food technology and the whole term was spent learning about balanced diets. Not once did the class attempt to cook!

Many educational practices derive from the assumption that students learn if given knowledge in spoken monologue or written two-dimensional form. You only have to look at the glazed, locked eyes of students to know this belief needs examining! Formal learning relies on verbal and written explanations. Remember the maxim of the famous Einstein: *Learning is experience. Everything else is just information.* Words are bits of data and a poor substitute for hands-on learning. Without active experience our images are distorted. Can you cook a wonderful meal just by reading the cookery book? No, of course not: it is making the dish that really teaches you how to cook. 'Knowing that' is only useful up to a point. 'Knowing how' is the real experience of learning something. Think about how you can make your activities with children as practical as possible. When I was head of an undergraduate medical sciences strand, the anatomy lecturer started vocal structure lectures by getting student pairs to make a paper larynx. This caught their imagination and helped them understand the complex components involved by engaging in talk with one another. This was different from my experience of fathoming the subject alone from Gray's Anatomy and a professor's words!

The limbic brain

The limbic brain includes the thalamus, hypothalamus, basal ganglia, amygdala and hippocampus. At about the age of 15 months, the limbic system adds emotion to the base patterns for sensory input and motor function. By five years, a child connects reason (from the cerebrum) with emotions and by eight adds insight (from frontal lobes) to refine thought. The intricate wiring of the limbic system shows that in order to remember and learn there must be strong input from the senses, a personal and emotional connection plus movement. This strongly supports experience-based learning. Gelernter (1994) makes the point that emotions are not a form of thought, or an additional way to think, but are fundamental to thought. Emotions, adding to the pain or pleasure of learning, are tied to body states so we think with our brains and bodies. Emotional development is responsible for our ability to absorb rules, values and wisdom and, without these intelligences, we can do little with our learning. Goleman (1996) has been influential in drawing our attention to this aspect in his splendid book, *Emotional Intelligence*.

The implications of these insights are enormous, especially to education. It is our emotions that mediate situations. Curriculum demands encourage us to deliver knowledge in segregated subject areas in an unemotional and unsociable environment. The connections to pupils' own personal concerns are usually remote. Teachers complain of being disciplinarians rather than educators as they clamp down on student emotional and social interactions. In many other countries, children do not start formal learning until age seven and have a school day that is a long morning, giving pupils a chance to develop their own interests as well as form links with the wider community. Our childcare and parental work patterns make this difficult to establish.

The cerebrum and cortex

The cerebrum and cortex comprise the largest brain structure. Put your hands together in loose fists with thumbs pointing downwards to get an idea of its size. Covering the cerebrum, like the peel of an orange, is the convoluted cortex, which is 2–5mm thick. It contains 20 billion nerve cells, using 0.85 litres of blood each minute and burning 400 calories daily. The brain functions by making an estimated one quadrillion (a million billions) brain cell connections. Merzenich (1995) observed that whenever we engage in new behaviour, the brain remodels itself. It retains this capacity throughout life as long as body and mind remain active. Even after brain damage, rewiring is possible to compensate for lost pathways. The harder we use the brain the more nerve connections are created. The two squashy left and right cerebral hemispheres, comprising the cerebrum, lie over the small cerebellum and only developed 100,000 years ago because of a need for language. There are four lobes:

- *frontal* (sequential movements including thoughts into speech);
- *parietal* (sensation and past experiences);
- *temporal* (interpretation);
- *occipital* (visual interpretation and association).

There is an incoming (sensory cortex) and outgoing area (motor cortex). The four lobes accept external information from the opposite side of the body. Information from the left ear goes into the right temporal lobe for interpretation whilst the right hand is controlled by the left motor cortex. All sensory-motor functions on the right side of the body are controlled by the left hemisphere and on the left the reverse usually occurs, although some people are transposed with at least part of the brain controlling the right side of the body and vice versa. The fact that some people use their right hand for writing and others their left is proof of brain differences. Knowledge is integrated, organised and reorganised through a bridge called the 'corpus callosum' which connects both hemispheres so that new experiences can be understood in the light of past memories.

What happens when children learn?

Children form images from sensory experience in the form of movements, feelings, tones, words, shapes and colours. The nerve networks connect these up from various parts of the brain. Movement patterns and emotional experiences are stored in the limbic system, tones and words in the temporal and frontal lobes, whereas shape and colour are in the occipital lobes.

When we hear the word 'bus' all our experiences of it are immediately available as images. We might picture a large, noisy, smelly, dangerous, heavy, brightly coloured, large-wheeled vehicle and recall memories of riding in buses with feelings of fright or fervour, with love or hate emotions about them. Do you remember the nursery song 'The wheels on the bus go round and round', which children accompany with circular arm movements? Does this conjure up pictures in your mind? Using stored images in our memories we make sense of new learning and come up with fresh ideas.

How can you help this learning?

When children hear or read something, their brains actively put words into existing images for comprehension. If you cannot achieve these images it is difficult to understand. Imagery is vital to thinking and understanding and is strengthened through drama, role-play and imaginary experiences. Get children to close their eyes for 30 seconds and make a picture on an imaginary screen above their eyes. This is an excellent way of helping visualisation and tapping into their emotional feelings. They will create dark, sharp, angry images such as animals in cages, if they are disturbed and light, bright, happy ones, such as playing on the beach, if they are mentally stable. This is a useful way to take a child's emotional temperature and assess working potential. Ask pupils to visualise ideas and describe their pictures to stimulate both thinking and language. For example, if you are studying a book, get students to imagine a person, place or object and talk about it to others. This helps bring together activities of both sides of the brain. It is thought that the left brain is largely responsible for verbalising and the right one for visualising (Bell, 1991). Children who find learning difficult fail to bring their verbal and visual images together and need help and support to do so.

Hormones and their effects

Before leaving our discussion of physical development, we need to mention hormones and their effect on learning potential. Before birth the hormone androgen determines the child's sexual characteristics. After birth, males and females are essentially equivalent in the amount of sex hormones in the blood as far as we can presently test them! At this stage, the growth hormones come into play. The pituitary, thyroid, adrenal and pancreas glands develop before birth and their secretions govern a child's growth throughout development.

The role of hormones in puberty is complex. Rapid physical growth and the development of the reproductive systems and secondary sex characteristics are triggered and maintained by sharp increases in hormone levels. In girls, oestrogen increases and produces the menstrual cycle. In boys higher levels of testosterone lead to their reproductive system. Sex hormones are themselves triggered by activating hormones released by the pituitary gland and these stimulate a range of growth-related hormones in the body. The range of ages at which these changes occur is large and puberty can take place anytime between 10 and 17 years with heredity and environment playing some part. For example, malnutrition interferes with physical and mental growth. There is a large body of evidence (Tanner,1970) that suggests that children who are more rapid in physical growth are also advanced in mental growth. They score better on intelligence tests and do better in school than more slowly developing peers. This is partly explained by the fact that fast developers acquire an early confidence about themselves and may be treated differently by others. Bee (2000) points out that the largest children are most likely to be leaders.

Researchers have found a relation between physical maturation and personality. Sheldon (1940) was the first to identify three body types:

- endomorphic (amount of fat – soft and round);
- mesomorphic (amount of muscle – squarely built);
- ectomorphic (length of bone – tall and thin).

Endomorphic boys were rated by teachers as assertive and aggressive; the mesomorphs were leaders and confident and quarrelsome; the ectomorphs were thoughtful, considerate but lacking in energy (Walker, 1962; Cortes and Gatti, 1965). Where do differences in teacher perceptions come from? One possibility is that society has a clear expectation about people and their body build. We expect muscular children to be athletic and energetic but the 'thin Jims' to be future professors. The first group will be encouraged in sport whilst the second might be propelled towards reading. Hormones, also, have effect on personality. Those with high concentrations of the male hormone are likely to be dominant and aggressive.

Learning and physical development

Motor skills depend on muscle and bone growth, and a child's unique rate of body and brain development may have profound influences on self-image and confidence. Physical growth sets limits on mental development. A child cannot do what her body is not developed to do and we are foolish if we expect her to. Physical readiness does not guarantee learning but is a necessary condition. Research suggests that children need opportunities to practise their emerging physical skills and we must reflect on whether our present educational system gives them sufficient opportunity. Obesity is growing in children as they spend more time sitting in front of a television than exercising their bodies (Sage, 2000). Fat Camps are now part of our holiday activity possibilities. This problem is exacerbated by huge media coverage of child abductions, which encourages parents to keep children indoors and less active whilst snacking on crisps, coke and chocolate.

Mental development

Perception, thinking and language are the mental activities of foremost importance in learning.

Perception

Perception is the meaning we attribute to the messages that reach our brains from our senses. School emphasises information that we see and hear and to a less extent to what we touch and feel. Total visual acuity is not reached until about age ten, but younger children have adequate sight for their needs. However, we must account for the fact that the fovea of the eye, dealing with two-dimensional material such as pictures and print, is not developed until after eight years. This has consequences for reading. We put more pressure nowadays on children reading, and Hunter-Carsch (1999) has mentioned high degrees of visual stress amongst pupils. It is perhaps significant that the ten countries with the top levels of pupil achievement all start school two years after we do in Britain. If children are ready to learn they are not exposed to damaging experiences of failure.

Hearing appears to improve steadily until adolescence: older children can hear and discriminate more high and low tones, soft and loud sounds, and sound levels not well discriminated by younger ones. Diorio et al (1993) have shown high levels of stress hormones such as adrenaline and cortisol in young children, which pass through the placenta from mother to child. These interfere with hearing development and are correlated with decreased learning and memory and increased attention problems. Levinson (1988) discovered that over 90 per cent of children with learning difficulties had ear infections as infants. This means large numbers of children miss hearing complex tones and are at risk for spoken and written language difficulties. With regard to hearing and vision, there is research to suggest that young children of about three years of age are more sensitive to contrasts and contours than older ones. Later, the child probably focuses more on objects, their uses and meaning, and less on auditory and visual contours.

Young children are not able to discriminate the location of touch like older ones (Sage, 1990). A standard way to measure this is to touch a child in two places at once. Younger children often only report one touch whilst older ones are reliable in spotting both, and errors are rare. It appears that there is not equal sensitivity over the bodies of young children.

Perceptual constancy, object concept and identity

A collection of skills called 'constancies', 'concepts' and 'identities', are vital to the learning process and develop within the first three years of life. When someone walks away from you, the image of that person becomes smaller on the retina of the eye but you see him or her as the same size. This demonstrates size constancy. A skill needed for this is depth perception. Next time you are in an airplane take a look at things on the ground. People and cars look like midgets and toys. As there is no way to estimate distance, size constancy cannot be maintained. You know their real size but they look smaller. Ability to recognise that shapes are the same, even though you are looking at them from a different angle, and that colours are, even though the amount of light or shadow may change, are other forms of constancy. Children have to learn the fact of constancy and continuity in themselves.

In addition to constancy, two facets of object concepts are learnt. First, children must understand that an object exists even when they cannot see or feel it, as when someone goes from the room or a toy is put away. This is known as 'object permanence'. Finally, a child must realise that objects retain their individual identity from one encounter to the next. When someone disappears and then returns they are the same person. This understanding is known as 'object identity' and animate (living) objects appear to be recognised before inanimate ones (Bell, 1970). This illustrates the intricate interconnections between the development of perception and relationships between people. Positive, responsive relationships with others influence any other relationships that the child is involved in. Supporting children who have not developed positive relationships needs time, patience and a calm approach and it often falls to the teaching assistant to deal with these difficult issues.

Attention

A great deal of research has been devoted to the pattern of attention. What are the child's preferences? How does he attend? Things that are moderately novel are most attended to, because the child has to assimilate new to old (Piaget, 1964). Initially, attention is for the whole figure and from age two months a process of decentering occurs whereby the child shows less concentrated focus on single objects or parts of a picture or object. Kagan (1971) points out the rules change as the child gets older as they are able to interpret differences and form hypotheses. Underlying attention is the idea of expectation. Cooper et al (1978) suggest six stages of attention, useful for teaching:

- 1–2 years: distractible: momentary attention;
- 2–3 years: concentrates for a time: on task of his own choice;
- 3–4 years: attention for one input only: can't listen if involved in task. Needs adult to set attention focus;
- 4–5 years: attention still for one input only: can attend under his own control;
- 5–6 years: attention for two inputs: can assimilate information whilst engaged in tasks;
- 6–7 years: integrated attention: established and maintained.

Gibson (1969) suggests optimisation of attention is guided by the following principles:

- captured to voluntary: attention 'captured' by things, which later becomes voluntary;
- unsystematic to systematic search: focus on bits only and later the whole;
- broad to selective: from the whole can select parts;
- inability to ignore irrelevancies to ability to do so: shuts out unwanted information.

The trend is towards more voluntary attention control, but many entering school have not achieved Cooper's integrated attention or Gibson's third and fourth dimension, so learning is slowed.

REFLECTION POINT 12 [2.9] [3.2.3]

- Use the Cooper or Gibson guide to work out the child's attention level and then try to encourage the next stage using time targets (one minute, then two minutes and so on).

Differences in perceptual development

Although there is variation in the rate at which perceptual skills are acquired, generally the child's chronological age is the best predictor. There are, however, interesting differences in style and preference. Kagan (1965) suggested children differ in conceptual tempo. Some, confronted with something new, pause and examine it carefully and quietly whilst others become excited and active and do not observe it for as long. This reflective/impulsive style appears stable and the reflective child has an easier time learning to read. Witkin (1962) observed the same phenomena with older children and adults.

More of the child's perceptual skills are present at birth than was previously thought but the role of experience and learning cannot be underestimated. There are few consistent sex differences in perception but girls appear less tolerant of pain and more sensitive to taste. No social class differences have been found but older, poorer children are more likely to be impulsive in their visual scanning of information and less successful learners.

Thinking

There are two major strands to research on thinking:

- those devising intelligence tests;
- those interested in stages of development and learning strategies.

Intelligence testing

Two Frenchmen, Binet and Simon (1916), published the first intelligence tests in 1905 to predict school success. The rationale was that people differ in brightness or ability and that this could be measured on verbal and non-verbal tests. The intelligence quotient (IQ) is based on a comparison of actual age (chronological age) with mental age. The formula is: mental age divided by chronological age x100 = IQ. A child with the chronological age of five, who solves all the problems for five and six-year-olds but nothing above this level has an IQ of 120: 6 divided by 5 × 100 = 120. A child of six with a mental age of four would have an IQ of 67: 4 divided by 6 x 100 = 67.

Such tests measure a limited number of thinking skills in an arbitrary fashion and do not indicate where the person is at in development. They do tell us something about performance in comparison to peers and predict school success with some reliability. Test scores are influenced by the child's heredity, although it is not clear which factors affect performance. Environment plays a major role. Whilst children inherit a range of potential abilities, where they will actually function within that range depends on the kind of environment they grow up in. Those offering secure, happy experiences and positive encouragement, facilitate maximum growth but others are depressing, limited and uninspiring, and inhibit development.

Research has shown that children from middle-class families who value learning test higher on standard tests. Regardless of social class, parents who provide appropriate play experiences, interact with their child, and offer love, support and expect success, tend to have children who score well on tests. Interventions, such as all-day enriched day care from infancy, have positive effects on scores. Children with high scores are likely to be those who explore and experiment and are independent and assertive. They are often first-born children who receive undivided adult attention. There are no real sex differences although males score higher in spatial ability and mathematical reasoning, whereas females test better on verbal reasoning and vocabulary tests. Test scores are very influenced by specific situations such as health and conditions of testing.

Comment

Many people feel uneasy about assigning a number to a child's performance. Traditional tests favour those who have good language abilities but Gardner's (1983) multiple intelligences theory (logical/mathematical, linguistic, visual spatial, bodily kinaesthetic, musical, interpersonal and intrapersonal) gives value to a wider range, including the skill of communicating well with others.

Nevertheless, the intelligence test movement has demonstrated the effects of secure, supportive, stimulating learning environments and allowed standard comparisons between performances. Tests can be a useful part of a larger assessment scheme, providing quantitive evidence to judge ability.

Thinking development

The sequence of development, which appears in general outline to be the same for all children, can be broken down into four periods. Piaget (1969), Bruner (1966) and Vygotsky (1962) are the influential psychologists in the child development field.

The stages in thinking development are set out below.

STAGE	AGE (YEARS)	NAMES GIVEN TO STAGE			DESCRIPTION	NOTES
		PIAGET	BRUNER	VYGOTSKY		
1	0–2	Sensori-motor	Enactive	Pre-language	Interactions are sensory and. active: seeing, hearing, reaching, touching, grasping, sucking. Reflexes and chance govern exploration, with movements not intended or planned.	Movement from reflexive to intentional behaviour. No internal representation of the world.
2	2–6	Pre-operational	Iconic	Represent-ational	Begins to represent objects/events in words but reasoning is limited to own desires (egocentric/self-centred). At six the child starts to de-centre and think beyond himself.	Thinking egocentric. Reasoning less tied to specific experience. Classifies objects and concepts.
3	6–11	Concrete operations	Symbolic	Creative Language	Manipulates representations as in ordering events. Says what he sees (rehearsal) to aid memory.	Makes complex classifications. Performs operations like addition, subtraction and ordering on actual experience/objects.

▶

STAGE	AGE (YEARS)	NAMES GIVEN TO STAGE			DESCRIPTION	NOTES
		PIAGET	BRUNER	VYGOTSKY		
4	11 +	Formal operations	–	–	Uses complex mental operations on things that he has experienced and searches systematically for solutions to problems.	Shifts from inductive (reasoning from facts) to deductive (reasoning from principles): 'If all men are equal, then you and I must be equal.' Systematic in exploration and search. Thinks about thinking.

Stages in thinking development

Comment

Piaget's theory is influential, but criticisms can be levied against it. Children do not develop at the same rate and this is not addressed. They are not at a given stage on every task or in every situation, which suggests some inconsistency in the stages. Some ages for activities may not be accurate. Borke (1975) reports that three to four-year-olds are less egocentric (self-centred) than Piaget maintains. Nevertheless, there is general support for a gradual progression of thinking through a fixed sequence of skills and discoveries. In those over three, there is evidence that middle-class children are a year or two more advanced than those from poorer environments. Analyses of mother–child interactions show that aspects of early stimulation such as the variety and complexity of toys and the amount the child is talked with and stimulated may hasten or retard mental development. No sex differences in rate of progress have been consistently found (Yarrow et al, 1972).

> ### REFLECTION POINT 13 [2.2] [3.2.1] [3.2.2]
>
> - Think of a child you are involved with and consider his/her development against the appropriate Piaget stage. How does their performance fit? Is this below or above actual age?

Language

Learning and teaching is a communicative experience in which information is constantly being exchanged between participants. In school, spoken and written words are the important medium. Consider this conversation between a teacher and six-year-old Mark. What patterns can you detect? [2.5] [3.2.2]

> Teacher (teaching a lesson on conservation, using two balls of modelling clay): *Mark, hold these two balls and tell me whether there is the same amount of clay in each.*
>
> Mark: *Yeh.*
>
> Teacher: *Now, I'm going to change one of the balls into a sausage shape, like this.* (Shapes one of the balls into a sausage shape in front of Mark.) *Is there the same amount of clay in both?*
>
> Mark: *Um, umm.* (Nodding his head)
>
> Teacher: *If you put it back into the ball, it would be the same.*
>
> Mark: *It would be the same.*
>
> Teacher: *It's longer and thinner, but I haven't added or taken any away so it must be the same amount.*
>
> Mark: *It's big around but is the same.*
>
> Teacher: *The ball is bigger around but shorter than the sausage, which is longer and thinner. They are different in shape but not in amount.*

Did you notice the following three patterns?

- **Expansions**: instances in which the adult repeats what the child has just said, expanding it into a complete adult grammatical sentence.
- **Imitations**: instances in which the child imitates what the adult has just said either exactly or with some simplification so that his sentence is less complex.
- **Reinforcement**: responses by the adult to the form of the child's answer.

During conversations, adults are not only giving children information, but also helping them structure their ideas through language.

How do children develop language?

There are several theories about language development, which are worth examining as many of our support strategies are based on them.

Imitation

The most obvious theory is that language results from the child's imitation of adults. However, children's language is unique and creative from the beginning and they do more reducing of what they hear than straight imitating. Since so much of what children hear is imperfect language, the imitation theory cannot be a complete explanation but there is no doubt that it plays a part, especially in early stages when infants often repeat what they hear.

Reinforcement

The second alternative is that children are shaped into language by some reinforcement pattern. Although reinforcement principles apply to aspects of language, particularly pronunciation, there is no evidence that it is systematically applied to all grammar learning.

Analysis

A third alternative places emphasis on ability to analyse adult language patterns and extract rules from them, which children copy and simplify for their own use. There is some truth in this because when you tell a child a story to be retold, they do so in a simplified way to match their level of thinking and language. Such analyses, however, are well beyond that of infants.

Language acquisition device

There has been much interest in the idea that children are born with a tendency to sort and learn rules for language 'transformations'. Chomsky (1965) proposed that sentences have an essential meaning (deep structure) and this is transformed by rules into a specific sentence (surface structure). For example, supposing the deep structure is: *Mark likes pears*, transformational rules can turn this into a question, *Does Mark like pears?* or passive question, *Are pears liked by Mark?* and so on. This is an enormously complex theory but it makes sense that children have some inbuilt system for dealing with the language that they hear.

No one alternative provides a comprehensive theory of language development, accounting for all that is observed or dealing adequately with word meaning. There is agreement, however, that there is a biological underpinning to language learning and a structure for sound and sentence development in English, which is outlined below.

LIP	TONGUE (FRONT)	TONGUE (BACK)
0–1 year: first words with much individual variation		
1–2 years: p b m w	t d n	
2–2.5 years: p b m w	t d n	k g ng h
2.5–3.5 years: p b m f w	t d n s y l	k g ng h
3.5–4.5 years: p b m f v w	t d n s z y l	k g ng sh ch j h
4.5 + years: p b m t v w	t d n s z th y l r	k g ng sh ch j h
5–6 years: th	r	
6–7 years: blends: tw tr dr pl str shr spl		

Development of the sound system of English

You will find that some children have not acquired the sound system by seven years and, if this is the case, there will be problems acquiring word-building skills for reading and spelling.

The development of word patterns is outlined below.

APPROXIMATE AGE	FEATURE	EXAMPLE
1–2 years	Two word combinations No sense of word order	*car nice* *biscuit want*
2–3 years	Three word combinations Talk about the present only	*He lose shoe.* *Where lady go?* *Give mummy cup.*
3–4 years	Four word combinations Use of statements, questions, comments Associate ideas: (knife and fork) Many words left out in a sequence	*Luke kicking ball now.*
4–5 years	Uses co-ordinating words (*and, but, so*) and connectives (*because, where*) Uses five attributes to describe (shape, name, colour, size, feel etc.)	*I like chocs but I don't like spinach.* *Round ball. It's blue, big and squashy.*
5–6 years	Uses language beyond the immediate situation. Orders ideas in some way	Q. *If baby falls what does Mummy do?* A. *She picks him up and puts a plaster on if he is hurt.*
6–7 years	Tells back information with about half the details correct. Uses features to connect up talk: *then, after, before, however* Replays events in the past – a holiday or weekend	

Development of word patterns (syntax)

REFLECTION POINT 14 [2.2] [3.2.1] [3.2.2]

- Can you think of a child that you know in the 1–7 age range? Do they match up with the language guidelines?

The previous section introduces the idea of a developmental structure for sounds and sentence formation, but acquiring these abilities does not mean that a child can use them. In order to cope with the large amount of talk that happens in school a child must have the following conversational moves (Sage, 2000).

Checklist of conversational moves

Can the pupil:

- Answer a closed what, who, when, where question demanding a specific response?

- Contribute an idea (even if not entirely appropriate) showing turn-taking ability?
- Listen and respond, showing maintenance moves such as eye contact for 75 per cent of the time, smiling, nodding, etc.?
- Answer an open how or why question demanding an explanation?
- Initiate a new idea in conversation that fits in with the topic under discussion?

If all moves are in place, this indicates an ability to follow either a spoken or written narrative. Listening with a forward posture and maintained eye contact suggests concentration and co-operation in exchanges. If attention wanders, it is a sign that the listener is bored or finds the information presented in an unhelpful way or above their level of discourse ability. Answering open questions demands ability to express cause and effect and link events. *Baljit, why are you drinking milk? Because I like it better than orange.* This linking of events clearly is the base for putting together information in talk or text. Initiating a new idea shows ability to connect ideas logically within the overall theme. It demands an overview of the situation and an understanding of the parts that fit together and make a whole (top-down and bottom-up processing). Don't assume that children have these moves on starting school. Many secondary pupils have problems with the why and how questions and cannot follow the lesson narrative easily, make explanations or give instructions. Skills and enterprise briefings suggest communication is the weakest ability in the workplace.

Comment

The rate of language development differs considerably from one child to the next and I have seen students in secondary schools whose use of language is only at the level of a five-year-old. They can chat, but have problems following the connected discourse of instruction and explanation and making a coherent response. Language development has occurred but narrative has fallen behind, probably in a large number of cases because of restricted opportunities to use language in a variety of ways. Narrative also has a developmental structure (Sage, 2000):

- Record – produce ideas;
- Recite – order ideas in a limited way but not in a time sequence;
- Refer – compare ideas;
- Replay – sequence ideas in time;
- Recount – explain ideas (Why? How?);
- Report – discuss ideas – giving an opinion;
- Relate – tell a story with setting, events, actions, reactions.

This is a guide to how we develop our ability to deal with a number of ideas and it is not difficult to understand the close relation between narrative ability and thinking. Bruner and others (1966) suggest language and thought are separate until about the age of six. They then come together as an aid to memory, problem solving and analysis. Dale (1976) suggests that mastering the linguistic system is not the same thing as putting it to work. Language is not used for many functions to memory, classification, and inner speech – until a point in development considerably later than the essential mastery of structure. Putting language to work is what developing narrative is about, but school puts a brake on talk and does not easily facilitate development of thinking and language.

How can you help?

Use the guides to sound, sentence and narrative structure to work out where your pupil/s fall on the developmental continuum. Try to encourage progress towards the level above by modelling this yourself so pupils hear the structures, but do not put pressure on them to achieve these until they spontaneously do so. For example: if the child has all the sounds up to the five-year stage but is not at the five to six year level of pronouncing *th* and *r* correctly, try to use words with these sounds in them so the child has plenty of opportunity to hear them, but do not require him to repeat the words until he appears to want to do so. Similarly, with sentences – if a child is using language to talk about the past and future they should be encouraged to hear stories and tell them back. With regard to narrative, the test is to see if a child can describe a number of things about an object. This is the beginning of narrative expression.

Emotional development

Life is a comedy for those who think and a tragedy for those who feel.
(Horace Warpole)

Mrs Brown was telling Mark off for kicking Kirsty in the playground. He responded angrily by shouting: 'I don't care!' as his eyes momentarily filled with tears.

Mark is showing with his tears that his heart is sad even if his head is saying words to the contrary. These two minds, the emotional and rational, operate in tight harmony for the most part. Feelings are essential to thought and vice versa. When passions surge, however, the balance tips and the emotional mind takes the upper hand, with the cortex deferring to the limbic system (see previous discussion of the brain processes). The connections between the limbic structures and the cerebral cortex, through a small almond-shaped part called the amygdala, strike a balance between head and heart, thought and feeling. An important aspect of learning is how to deal with your emotions. Albert Camus (*The Plague*) has the answer as to who teaches us to cope with these: *The reply came promptly: Suffering.* Dealing with emotions is a painful business.

Of concern to teachers is the child's aggression and attachment (dependency). The earliest patterns of interactions between carer and infant seem to be a kind of 'dance' in which the child signals with eye contact, smiles and chuckles and the adult responds. Attachment to the child may be affected by the ability of the pair to achieve satisfactory communication with one another.

There are clear sequences in the development of attachments going from diffuse to single and then multiple attachments (Ainsworth, 1973). In older children there is a shift away from dependent behaviours such as clinging, holding and touching toward mature forms such as seeking attention and approval. Children differ in the strength and quality of their early attachments and the speed in which they pass from immature to mature forms of dependency. Consistency in dependent behaviour is more notable in females than males and is the reason why there are more boys in school with emotional and behaviour problems. Individual differences are partly determined by care practices, although the child's temperament (discussed earlier under physical development) may be influential. Among older children the degree of dependency seems to be jointly determined by the amount of reward and punishment that adults provide in response to the child's bids for dependency.

Developmental trends in aggressive behaviour are less clear than for attachment, but suggest shifts from physical to verbal aggression, as the child gets older (Goodenough, 1931). Individual differences appear marked, with boys showing more physical aggression (probably because of their strength and hormones) at all ages. Consistency in aggression through life is more apparent in males than females. There is reason to suppose that the baby comes equipped with a link between frustration and aggression, as this is such a common response in all children. Other responses to frustration can be learnt. Some child-rearing practices have been consistently linked with high levels of aggression and these include rejection, high levels of physical punishment, and a combination of permissiveness and punishment. The context for emotional development is vital and Erikson (1963) highlights this in his eight stages of emotional maturity.

Erikson's stages of maturity are:

- Early infancy: trust versus mistrust;
- Late infancy: autonomy versus shame and doubt;
- Early childhood: initiative versus guilt;
- Middle childhood: competence versus inferiority;
- Adolescence: identity versus role confusion;
- Early adulthood: intimacy versus isolation;
- Middle adulthood: production versus stagnation;
- Late adulthood: self-acceptance versus despair.

Stages are based on a series of contrasts. As the child, adolescent, young and old adult experience life, they develop positive or negative concepts of themselves in relation to what happens to them. For example, if the young infant sets up good communicative relationships with others he will learn trust, but if they are bad, mistrust occurs. Erikson proposes a growth pattern of constructs, which slot into other learning. When the child is in school and able to compare his performance against others, he starts to grasp an idea of his competence in relation to them. If he sees himself doing worse than his peers, feelings of inferiority will be experienced and learnt. Sage (2003) argues that these abstract concepts, based on fundamental notions of good and bad, are the way a child analyses the world. All early experience such as feeding and care generate good or bad feelings for the child. These become the base measure for judging succeeding events.

Clearly, the concept of self that emerges from experiences includes both the children's view of themselves (self-concept); their body and abilities (self-image) and their degree of self-esteem (value for self). The earliest stage is the discovery that they are separate from others, constant and continuous. By the age of two children have learnt their own name and by three have achieved a measure of autonomy as a result of developing physical, mental, social and emotional skills. At four, children show possessiveness about their space and things and by five to six can verbalise thoughts and emotions and form positive or negative judgements about themselves. Meadows (1993) reminds us, however, that children cannot be relied on to express accurately their feelings as it takes many years to identify and communicate these. Children with low esteem are anxious and have more difficulties coping with school. Those with high esteem have their achievements valued and praised and experience a warm relationship with clear communication and limits set on behaviour (Merry, 1998). Men are more confident in new tasks, but this may well change as women take on more leading roles in society.

How can we support emotional development?

In schools, we are learning to take a child's emotions more seriously and terms such as 'emotional literacy' allude to the importance of attending to the feelings of pupils. Research on emotional development and self-concept suggests that the communicative relationship between the child and others is the key to successful learning. In our relationships with others we learn what they think of us and, even if this is not communicated in words, it most definitely will be in actions such as tone of voice, facial expressions and gestures. Wragg (1994) reminds us that in schools, four out of five comments to children are negative and we can make a conscious effort to reverse this and ensure that feedback is largely positive.

Social development

No man is an island, entire of itself.

(John Donne, 1624)

Children are born into a society of others and socialising them into its norms are major tasks. There are five theories, which we will skip through. None of them account adequately for developmental patterns and individual differences but are useful reference points for our attitudes and views.

The ethological theory (Bowlby, 1969)

This emphasises inborn, instinctive patterns of interaction. The child provokes care by cries and movements and prolongs it with smiles and chuckles. With development, the instinctive patterns come under the child's control. Attention is focused on the patterns of interaction that the child appears to naturally bring with him into the world.

The psychoanalytic approach 1 (Freud, 1960)

This concentrates on instinctive behaviour of self-preservation, particularly with reference to sex. At each stage sexual energy ('libido') is invested in a specific part of the body ('erogenous zone') and the maturational shift is triggered by changes in sensitivity of the different regions. The stages are 0–1 years: oral (mouth),1–3 years: anal (bottom), 3–5 years: phallic (genitals), 5–12 years: latency (resting period with own sex relationships), 12–18 years: genital (sexual energy). The important event in the phallic stage is the 'Oedipal conflict' in which the boy becomes aware of his mother as a sex object and competes with father. The conflict is resolved when he identifies with his father and represses feelings for his mother. For a girl the conflict is different as the original attachment is to her mother with a shift to her father. The broad outline of the development of attachments is accepted but not the dynamics of the process.

The psychoanalytic approach 2 (Erikson, 1963)

This approach focuses on changes in the child's motor and cognitive skills and the impact these have on interactions. The eight stages have been described in the previous section. This theory has been influential because it brings together mental and personality development and accounts for individual differences in interactions.

Social learning theories (Bandura et al, 1973)

These theories emphasise that the child's way of interacting with others is learned. Attachment is based on having needs met repeatedly with good things so that the child begins to see the people who provide them as positive. Obviously, children's responses are influenced by the way people respond to them. Children do learn in ways that please adults and from observing models.

Cognitive-developmental theories (Kohlberg, 1966)

The essential tenet of this approach is that the behaviour of a child is the result of his mental level. Changes in attachments are seen as the result of shifts in thinking ability.

Comment

Each theory offers a particular strength. The ethological theory tells us about early interaction, whilst the social learning concepts help us to understand what happens over the childhood years. The cognitive-developmentalists point out the critical mental underpinnings to relations with others. Erikson's psychoanalytic theory combines several of these threads. The theories do not clarify the nature of a child's social interaction at home and school. Outside class a child has many one-to-one and small-group exchanges, which are informal in nature and not judged as right or wrong responses. In these interactions it is usually the child who asks the questions and the adult who gives the answers. The child has opportunity to control the exchange. In school, the opposite occurs, with adults continually questioning and requiring correct answers and children only allowed to talk at the teacher's direction. Children are forced into a passive role and easily become anonymous within the large class group. Teacher assistants have a great opportunity to work with children in one-to-one situations or small groups and can give pupils some control over the exchange and help to balance the large-class situation. Paulo Freire (1972) describes the ideal class interaction for successful learning, which replaces the teacher as the *sage on the stage* with a *guide by the side!*

SUCCESSFUL CLASS INTERACTION [1.1] [3.3.2]

- Think about the following points and how they help build successful interaction in the classroom:

  - Students express themselves so that they can hear each other's voice and opinions (even if it just saying their name);

  - Space is allowed for external input from teacher or another expert on the topic;

  - Dialogue takes place in pairs, small groups or large groups (depending on size) to reflect on the input;

  - Students summarise the dialogue (in pairs or groups) and record their summary if necessary.

This model gives greater control over learning to the pupil and, if valued and practised, produces much more able, interested and committed children, who view themselves as active participants in the process. The National Curriculum has made teachers' discourse the order of the day as they monopolise class talk in order to thrash through prescribed topics. It is worth remembering that you can only really communicate effectively if there is some equality in the interaction. This is the rule outside school but not inside, and many pupils are frustrated by that fact.

Roles

Traditional theories also say very little about roles in social interaction and how these affect the exchange. A role is a part a person plays within a given group and situation. The part requires certain kinds of behaviour, which defines the person's relationship with others in the group. For example, within the family you may have the part of oldest daughter, sister, niece and cousin.

Custom gives you special responsibility as your parents view you as a pillar of strength in all family affairs and you expect to be taken into their confidence. As an older sister you feel responsible for your younger sisters and brothers. So each of these roles in the family entitles you to certain rights but involves obligations too. Our positions determine whether we are a leader or follower in a group and give different opportunities to learn social skills.

Each of us plays many roles in the course of our lives as Jacques said in *As You Like It: All the world's a stage, and all the men and women merely players; they have their exists and their entrances and one man in his time plays many parts* (Act 2, scene 7). Social scientists have attempted classifications of these parts. Basic roles depend on sex, age, position in the family and class, none of which is ours through merit. Occupational roles are largely achieved through our own merits and may include the parts children play in school. If you are viewed as physically, mentally, emotionally and socially able you are likely to be assigned leading roles, offering you greater opportunities than others demonstrating less abilities. If you reflect on the different roles you play they might produce the following array:

Family roles	Social roles	Work roles
Daughter/son	friend	teacher assistant
Sister/brother	acquaintance	part-time student
Cousin	team-mate	other part-time jobs
Grand-daughter/son	member of a sports club	
Aunt/uncle	member of a drama, social or music group, etc.	

Life roles

In our social life, there is some choice as to which role we adopt, and we have to take account of the situation itself, the other person and ourselves. Situations prescribe roles very clearly. Your friend is in hospital, recovering from an operation, and in your visitor role you are expected to bring comfort and support and the customary grapes and flowers! What about other situations? Your role will depend on a variety of factors and be influenced by things like age, gender, kinship, class and occupation. In school, you will have a role to play with colleagues, children and their parents. What are your expectations and how does your teacher assistant role influence how others respond to you? Pupils will see you as an authority figure, but since your role is likely to be more intimate than that of a class teacher, they will view you more like a parent, with a special, personal relationship with them. However, you have teaching functions that expect children to respond to you correctly, which produces more tension and stress in the relationship.

Finally, the role you choose depends on your own self-image and at the beginning of any social encounter two people negotiate over the roles they adopt. Our relationships are more harmonious if we make clear our role and accept those played by others. If a colleague is playing the earnest expert and you persist in finding him funny, then the interaction will collapse.

Your choice of role has many consequences. It affects how you dress, the way you speak and are spoken to and the kinds of rights or obligations you may expect, the sort of people you might encounter and so forth. If you regard yourself as an educated sophisticate, you will dress smartly and attractively, and talk about serious ideas with others and expect to be invited to courses and lectures rather than football matches!

Understanding and diversifying our roles is an important part of our development. Children in school play many parts, not only learner but also class star, fool or troublemaker, etc. Some roles may deflect from children's primary role as learner. Sage (2000: 25) expands on this and looks at examples of children with learning problems and how their role as poor learners deprives them in subtle ways of many opportunities to learn. Small children play adult roles of mothers and fathers or doctors and nurses to reach some understanding of what it is like to be in these positions. Role-play is an important technique in learning. To adopt an unfamiliar role demands empathy so you might see an antagonist such as a parent, teacher, and policeman in a new light and avoid conflicts. As a teacher assistant, try to make sure children experience working in many different groups that give them opportunities to play leader and follower roles. Also reverse roles in a task so they are teaching you what they have learnt and can appreciate your part in the learning with greater understanding.

Supporting child development within the inclusive philosophy

In the last 25 years, since the Warnock Report (1978) into the education and management of children and young people with special educational needs (SEN), we have radically shifted our views regarding the way we educate our children. Before 1978 we believed that children learnt best in segregated settings with others of similar ability. The Warnock report extolled the virtues of all children being educated together so that they understood diversity. After the Education Act 1981, the policy became to integrate SEN pupils into mainstream settings where possible, but this did not mean they were always fully included in curriculum activities. For example, children with physical impairments would often find themselves spectators rather than participators in active learning situations such as sport, drama, food technology and science experiment sessions.

Inclusion is often described as a journey away from segregation (Bennett et al, 1998:155). Traditionally, pupils with particular difficulties have been put together with others whose needs are similar in either units or schools where specially trained staff and facilities are available. Such children are segregated, therefore, from neighbourhood friends, which can be stigmatising for them and deprive them of a full range of educational opportunities.

In recent years reports have raised questions about the desirability of segregating special education from mainstream schooling (Warnock, 1978). These became embodied in the Salamanca World Statement issued by the United Nations Educational, Scientific and Cultural Organisation (UNESCO) (1994:11) on principles, policy and practice in SEN: *Inclusion and participation are essential to human dignity and to the enjoyment and exercise of human rights.*

Government has supported the principle of equalisation of educational opportunity as a result of the Salamanca agreement. The shift in emphasis from an exclusive focus on individual pupil needs to one centring on the skills and resources in mainstream schools is the difference between integration and the more recent concept of inclusion.

Children are educated against a background of constantly shifting circumstances, so the list below defines the terms that describe difference, such as gender, race, social class, culture, ethnicity, disability, special educational needs and special/additional needs. Additionally, comments need to be made about the problems in using these terms, as they are often a focus for debate and dissension.

- **Gender** is the male or female classification according to the physical attributes of each. Male/female stereotypes often dictate how boys and girls are treated and are frustrating for many children.
- **Race** is a biological concept, classifying people by common origin and broad physical features. It is a word that throws up typical stereotypes and false assumptions.
- **Social class** defines families on the basis of parent occupation according to the Registrar General's classification. There has been some blurring of the categories with the move from industrial to service occupations and more school leavers now entering higher education.
- **Culture** encompasses the traditions and lifestyle shared by members of a society, including their ways of thinking, feeling and behaving. The term assumes an unjustifiably high level of homogeneity and cohesion among the members and different family patterns add to the complexity of pupils' backgrounds.
- **Ethnicity** reflects membership of a distinctive social group. Distinguishing features include physical appearance, language, religious beliefs and practices, national allegiance, family structure and occupation (Thomas, 1994). The term fixes on particular aspects of identity and ignores others that might be important. Children from mixed marriages and those living in countries where they are not native often have difficulties with identity.
- **Disability** describes someone who has impairment such as vision or hearing loss that renders them less able to perform normally. The term

assumes a person rather than a situation centred approach. For example, wheelchair users may be viewed as having mobility problems but equally could be seen as hampered by inappropriate building design.

- **Special educational needs (SEN)** signify a child with learning difficulties that call for particular provision. Learning difficulties are those beyond the average for age and may result from disabilities (DfEE, 1996, section 312). In practice, the term can be divisive as such children become subject to the code of practice arrangements that set them apart from their peers (the *Revised SEN Code of Practice*, DfES, 2001).

- **Special/additional needs** define a child from a social group whose circumstances or background are different from most of the school population. Language, culture, overt racism and socio-economic disadvantage are identified as special/additional needs without any implication that individual pupils may have learning difficulties in the same sense as SEN (Robson, 1989). The term is frequently confused with SEN, resulting in low expectations of this group of pupils and confusion in planning support.

REFLECTION POINT 15 [1.1] [1.2] [2.5] [3.3.3] [3.3.7]

Take a child in your class and locate the number of different groups to which she/he belongs, using the eight categories above. Which one/s produce/s difficulties for the child? How would you deal with these?

Baljit's story

Baljit was an Anglo-Indian eight-year-old with communication problems due to Otitus Media, a medical condition known as glue ear, where fluid is unable to drain from the middle ear region so preventing sound conduction. Although he had had grommets (draining tubes) inserted into the ear drum to assist draining these had not been successful. His English father had died and his maternal grandparents mainly cared for him whilst his mother worked to support Baljit and his two younger sisters. There was considerable tension amongst the grandparents due to differences in cultural rearing patterns. Speech problems produced most difficulty, closely followed by emotional insecurity due to family tensions. Baljit gained useful support at school from a teaching assistant, giving him the opportunity to discuss feelings and needs. He received weekly help from a teacher for the hearing impaired and made great progress as a result of belonging to a Communication Opportunity Group, which developed thinking and interaction to make the most of his abilities.

In modern society, people have complex identities and multiple roles so labels can be misleading. Discrimination detected in processes, attitudes and behaviour is common in minority groups and SEN children, and some ethnic groups, such as West Indians, figure high in figures for exclusion (Sage, 2004: 7-20). Teaching assistants get involved with the detail of children's lives and can often spot the problems that pupils are having because their differences present barriers to learning and social interaction. Being observant and aware and keeping a small notebook, to record incidents for later discussion with colleagues, enables support staff to play a crucial role in developing successful inclusive practices and preventing unpleasant incidences.

Summary

This chapter has attempted to overview the main ideas that underpin how children learn. There are many different theories about this. All are interesting and give us opportunities to reflect more closely on a very complex process in which children, with increasingly diverse circumstances, bring together their physical, mental, emotional and social development as the platform for their learning. There is a rough consensus that growth is a gradual process, based on innate potential and a positive environment. Many things can interfere with this development and there are large numbers of children who arrive in schools without a base to learn, and significant numbers who are excluded because educators cannot deal with them successfully. By considering theories of learning, within present inclusive philosophies, teaching assistants will have the knowledge and awareness to give the appropriate input to children and encourage interesting and worthwhile responses. These responses, perhaps, should not be judged as right or wrong but as a valuable contribution to a child's learning. Although it is not the remit, in a general text that provides merely an overview, to consider specific learning problems (see *A World of Difference: Tackling Inclusion in Schools*, Sage, 2004, for a comprehensive review of common learning and medical conditions in children) it is worth noting that interventions are generally based on developmental guidelines. Establishing a strong knowledge of how learning occurs, as a result of the child's natural development and the quality of stimulation and support around, is the best preparation for observing and assessing individual pupil needs and providing worthwhile experiences.

Take time to reflect on the main points that have been covered in this chapter.

- Learning has physical, mental, emotional and social components.
- Aspects of learning integrate to support each other's development.
- Growth is gradual and generally thought to follow a developmental course.
- Children achieve learning at different rates due to factors inside and outside the child.

- Learning requires good positive communication and support from adults.
- Teaching assistants have a unique opportunity to develop effective learning by giving children some control of the process through encouraging thinking and communication.
- Formal learning now takes place in an inclusive context, where educators need awareness and knowledge of the range of differences and the barriers these present to development.

3. The skills needed to support learning and behaviour

The teaching assistant's role supporting learning has brought a fresh focus to the activities of adults in the classroom. Let's ask Mina, a teaching assistant in a primary school, to give us a glimpse of her day.

Mina's story

Hello, I'm Mina. I work in a city primary school with 420 children, 14 teachers and six teacher assistants. Seventy per cent of our children speak English as a second language. I am Punjabi speaking myself but I married an Englishman so we do speak English at home. I left school with 4 GCSEs and went into a knitwear factory until I married and had two children. I became very interested in their learning and, after helping in a playgroup for two years, applied for this job. I have been in school for five years. I love every minute of it. The pay's not good but the rewards make me feel like a millionaire! There is nothing better than seeing children learn happily and knowing that you have played a vital part in that experience.

So what about my role? I work across Years 2 and 3 supporting two statemented children daily for an hour each. Baljit (Year 2) has understanding and expressive problems in Punjabi and English. Marcus (Year 3) has difficulties with attention for tasks. The rest of the day is spent supporting Year 2 and 3 classes, running a school book club and an after-school Communication Opportunity Group Scheme as part of our learning support initiatives. Let's look at a typical day as the starting point to consider what skills I need to do my job well.

8.30 a.m. – I arrive at school. Sue Tyler, the Year 2 teacher has a heavy cold and is almost voiceless! I send her to the staffroom for a 'cuppa' and with the help of the timetable set to and organise the classroom for the day. Sue has to see a worried mother so I welcome the children, speak to parents and carers, take the register and explain the day. It is very windy and everyone is ' high' and needs calming down. I put on some music and I get them to close their eyes while I tell them a story. This works!

9–10 a.m. – I take Baljit for special time in the library corner of the class, which is screened off from the rest of the space. Together with Sue and Rekha (special needs language teacher), we have devised a plan to help his understanding. I read a short story or poem and Baljit has to pick out the person, place and happening. We then draw these. He is now picking out the person and place. The strategy works well and we have some fun with our pictures! Today's poem is the 'Man on the Moon' who has a boil in his ear and rheumaticky knees. The knees were our problem! How can you explain this to a 7-year-old? We managed – using some gestures to show that walking is difficult if your joints are stiff and painful!

▶

10–10.30 a.m. – Sees me back in class helping those struggling with some tessellations! The children laugh when I get in a muddle but we work it out together by helping each other.

10.30–11.00 a.m. – I rush to open the bookshop and give out books to those who have brought money. By the end of break I have 30 separate amounts to add and record. There is only time for a quick coffee before being back in the class for literacy hour.

11.00–12.00 a.m. – Literacy hour finds me taking a small group of less able pupils in the plenary session. We are working on vocabulary and looking at some different meanings of the word 'fly', after a story about flying machines. We produce a colourful poster to record our ideas – everyone loved the tale of the old woman who swallowed a fly and she features boldly!

12.00–12.30 p.m. – Music time! We have chosen 'The Little Brown Jug' to sing and play to. The percussion is a bit too loud and I have to intervene. Tracy is in tears and I draw her aside for a quiet word and find her Mum was taken to hospital in the middle of the night. I make a note to tell other colleagues and ensure she gets support.

12.30–1.00 p.m. – There is a half-hour staff meeting on after-school clubs and I have to give a presentation on the Communication Opportunity Group Scheme. I have some video of sessions and progress is obvious. Everyone is so pleased and the talk goes well.

1.15 p.m. – I rush to Year 3 (my afternoon class) to prepare resources for some work on transport. The children have brought in toy models and I negotiate with them how to arrange these and then collect books and videos from the library.

1.30–2.30 p.m. – I take Marcus for his hour's coaching. We are working on attention and our target is ten minutes. We have a description of a friend to write and illustrate and both of us work out how best to get the task done. The ten-minute target was completed well and Marcus gets a merit point.

2.30–3.15 p.m. – I am out on the field with half of Year 3 and Mrs Brown has the other half. We are teaching them rounders. Some are not good at waiting their turn and we need to look at this. I discuss the problem with Mrs Brown on the way back to class.

3.15 p.m. – I take the class for a story and review the day's activities as Mrs Brown slips off to do a certificate course at the university. I see the children off and tidy up and at 3.45 p.m start COGS with a group of pupils from Year 2 and 3 who are well behind in thinking and communication and also badly behaved. We are on our third week of a ten-session course working at level 1 to develop and express ideas. The children love the activities and it is very worthwhile helping them access their learning more successfully. I have a PGCE student with me and have to explain what we are doing and why.

▶

> *4.40 p.m. – I negotiate with the head teacher to do an assignment observing class behaviour. He agrees but only after some strong persuasion! He does not seem to understand the level and demands of my course. I then go home. I have an assignment task on 'talking to children' for my University Teacher Assistant Award. I love to learn about the learning and teaching process as it gives me confidence to do my job.*

Do you feel exhausted reading about Mina's day? Stamina is the name of her game! Apart from a strong constitution what do you think her main skill is? Yes, you're right. It's good communication. How many different communication activities has Mina been involved in? Jot them down and then check your answers against the list in Appendix 3. [**1.6**]

Most people enter learning support with good informal skills in talking to others, but class talk is very different. It demands more formal, public uses of speaking. Instead of the unplanned content of most informal conversations, talk in class is about following a line of inquiry towards a learning goal. Participators must be focused, understand the goal and be able to put together events. Adults talk for at least two-thirds of the lesson time, giving lengthy instructions, explanations and information aimed at a mid-ability level. Many children cannot cope with vast quantities of talk and do not have the listening ability to bring together information. An important role of the support adult is to reinterpret what the teacher says in a way that a child can understand.

The skills of the support adult are listening to and counselling others, taking in a great deal of information quickly and frequently rephrasing it, using questions to help pupils think through a task, giving clear explanations and instructions, presenting information to colleagues at staff meetings and occasionally at a governors' meeting. In addition, there is a need to be well organised, take initiative (as when the teacher felt unwell), and work as a supportive team member. You have to be responsible working alone with individuals and groups, and know how to teach, control and counsel pupils and sometimes colleagues. Knowledge of the teaching and learning process is essential. The following tasks and tips have helped Mina learn the skills she needed, so how about trying them out?

Top tips for teaching assistants. Verbal and non-verbal skills

Top tip 1: Thinking about your role [1.2] [1.5] [3.3.2] [3.3.6]

In your employee role you have to accept, understand and carry out the policies and practice adopted by your school. This section considers some of the specific roles you need, as implementing learning is a process in which you have to talk and relate to others in various ways. There are four main components to adult communication in a classroom. Can you complete the table below? Line 1 provides an example of what is involved in listening, controlling, questioning and explaining. Think up some activities within these areas. Some answers are in Appendix 3.

LISTENING	CONTROLLING	QUESTIONING	EXPLAINING
hearing	instructing	requesting	informing

Components of adult communication in the classroom

Rate yourself to develop an idea of what abilities come easily to you and what need to be worked on. A = excellent, B = average, C = below average:

LISTENING   A   B   C
CONTROLLING   A   B   C
QUESTIONING   A   B   C
EXPLAINING   A   B   C

This helps you to think about how you use communication in the classroom. Now consider some of the skills needed by completing the checklist below. It has been compiled from research indicating areas important for classroom practice. Tick questions you answer 'yes' to and cross those where the reply is 'no'.

Establishing trust:

● Do you express your feelings easily and clearly?

● Do you allow pupils and colleagues to know what sort of person you are?

● Do you let pupils know you respect them?

● Do you give pupils routine, roles and responsibilities in the contexts in which you work?

Presenting a positive example:

● Do you come over as cheerful and confident?

● Do you treat pupils fairly and firmly and reward rather than punish?

● Do you use positive rather than negative commands?

● Do you make expectations clear and praise when these are met?

Supporting learning:

● Do you develop pupil's self-esteem and confidence?

● Do you differentiate tasks to suit needs?

● Do you help pupils to set goals and plan to meet these?

● Do you vary communication to suit the audience?

Listening:

- Do you listen without becoming distracted? ☐
- Do you visualise what you are hearing so that you remember? ☐
- Do you record key ideas? ☐
- Do you summarise what you have heard? ☐

Verbal behaviour:

- Do you address others in a polite, friendly way? ☐
- Do you adjust questions to suit a pupil's thinking and understanding level? ☐
- Do you give clear instructions and explanations? ☐
- Do you use words and sentences that others understand? ☐

Non-verbal behaviour:

- Do you use regular eye contact with those you talk to? ☐
- Do you use an expressive voice to help others attend to what you say? ☐
- Do you normally smile, look relaxed and appear pleasant? ☐
- Do you use facial expressions and gestures to support your words? ☐

Try the communication profile in Appendix 3 to see what your view is of yourself as a communicator. [1.2] [1.4] [1.5] [3.3.2]

Verbal skills

Listening to others

Listening uses our minds to pay attention to sound sensations and then makes meaning from them. It is a deliberate activity and is different from hearing, which is the automatic process of turning sound waves into sensations. In any conversation we find ourselves hovering between attending to the other person's words and to our own private concerns. We only truly listen attentively to about 12 per cent of what we hear and miss a great deal of what is said to us. We listen in short 30-second bursts before losing attention and many factors impair this activity. We switch off when bored, distracted and have more interesting thoughts to follow, or if we dislike the speaker's mannerisms, accent, appearance or personality. There are other constraints on our listening. For example, if messages follow too rapidly or we are trying to listen to two sources at the same time, it becomes impossible to follow the thread of talk.

So, let us consider ways in which listening can be improved. Try to pay attention to the key concepts in an event: the person/object, the place and the happening. Imagine what they are like by picturing them in your mind. The details then will become linked to these three pivots.

In interpersonal and counselling situations, practise empathetic listening, which means concentrating on the other person's concerns and seeing things from their point of view. If you give plenty of feedback (smiling, nodding, making appropriate, encouraging noises) you show you are listening. Practise the 'mirroring technique', in which you paraphrase what the speaker has said: *You are very upset that you were not chosen to go on the school trip.* This helps to affirm and clarify issues as well as indicating interest. It is an effective strategy to help problem solving.

Undoubtedly, you listen better if you have a good reason for doing so. Pupils listen when told about outings or holiday dates! If you are listening for a long time, getting actively involved in note taking and asking questions will keep you on track more effectively. Remember listening is the same as understanding. It is a higher thinking process that needs constant practice. Although it is our most frequent activity in the classroom we tend to give it very little attention in the teaching process.

Controlling talk

Much of the research on school misbehaviour suggests that pupils' two major problems are difficulties understanding adult language and their own problems with using communication effectively. In a small study of 100 pupils, I found that communication with adults was pupils' principal problem in school (Sage, 2000b). Try asking some children what they find most difficult about school. This will help to build your knowledge of how best to deal with them. [1.2] [3.2.3] Meanwhile, try and take on board some of the following information about effective talk.

Contact

Greeting pupils or colleagues with a smile and focused, relaxed eye contact is the way to establish a positive relationship. Badger (1992) found that adults are so pressurised with the demands of the National Curriculum in schools that proper greetings are overlooked and the treatment of pupils has become impersonal and functional. Making relationships properly reduces behaviour problems, as pupils feel cheated if they are not acknowledged in a friendly, personal way. This social talk is called 'phatic' communication and its purpose is to produce a warm feeling and a sense of belonging rather than information. Note how effective communicators indulge in this 'small talk' to relax everyone before getting down to real business.

- Greet your pupils warmly and express pleasure in having the opportunity to learn together.
- Make regular eye contact with those you talk to, remembering that we all tend to favour our dominant side (right, if left-handed and left, if right-handed) and ignore half our listeners.

Top tip 2: Clarity [1.2] [2.9] [3.3.4] [3.3.8]

Try these tips to clarify what you mean and deal effectively with difficult behaviour:

- Use 'I' statements: *Tom, I need you to listen* – is more effective than: *Tom you aren't listening.*
- Repeat statement, if ignored, in same voice – tone and volume shows firmness.
- Say how you feel: *Tom, I feel cross when you talk as I can't listen* – focus on you not them.
- Check understanding: *Tom, you said you didn't understand, is that right?* – clarifies.
- Interpret cause: *Tom, you're cross with me but not saying so* – establishes truth.
- Give positive feedback first: *Tom, thanks for listening. Now, I need you to finish this by break.*
- Compromise: *Tom, you didn't understand the lesson. Come and see me at 12.30 for help.*
- Control feelings: if angry – count to ten before speaking.
- Resolve conflict: *You're upset about this work. I need it done. Let's solve this together.*
- Make goal clear: clarify behaviour; state effect; refer to incident; allow space for response: *Tom, chatting in class annoys me. It means I can't hear the teacher talking. Can you listen silently so I can get the information to help you?*

Which of these strategies do you employ? Are there some you use less frequently? Can you explain why? A possible reason why pupils might not respond to your talk is because they are not clear what is meant by the words, facial expressions and gestures that you use. There is a need to be precise. *Listen silently* is clearer than *Listen quietly*. *Quietly* implies that talk is acceptable. Also, *Listen silently when the teacher is talking* is likely to produce a better response than *Don't talk while the teacher is speaking*. There is no negative vibe and the image is clearer.

Look at the following list of comments made to pupils by adults. Wragg (1994) has suggested we make five negative to one positive statement/s to pupils. Can you turn these negative comments into positive ones and make the message clearer and more acceptable to the receivers? [1.3] [2.9] [3.3.2]

That's very messy.	Jack, don't do that.
I'm fed up with your talking.	I'm not going to put up with this.
I'm not starting till you simmer down.	I'm not putting up with this behaviour.
This work won't do.	Don't pick your nose, Brad.
Do you want to stay in at break?	You are a bad boy, Tom.
I don't like your writing, Emma.	Don't run in the corridor.
This work is a disaster.	Don't whisper, Clare.
It's not good enough, class 10.	Can't you use your brains, Lee?
That's appalling.	Don't make such a fuss.
Don't bully.	When you've shut up, I'll start.
Matthew, are you always this lazy?	See me at break, Amy.

Consistency

Your school has a behaviour management policy. Thinking up rules and routines is the easy bit but implementing them throws us on the mercy of our fragile wills! We can say it but can we do it! Consistency is the hardest aspect of behaviour management. Keeping up the good work when we are tired, hard-pressed or one degree under needs iron will. Behaviour polices fail in schools not because their principles are wrong but because they are hard to adopt on a consistent basis. Everyone has a preferred way of maintaining discipline. You may not agree with your colleagues but all must sign up to an agreed policy as otherwise it is wasted and wearisome.

Top tip 3: Reframe requests positively [1.3] [2.9] [3.3.2] [3.3.4]

Pupils cannot be talked out of how they feel. Consistently say: *You find this boring but we must do it. You can do it now or give up your lunch break.* Choice gives control to the pupil and reframing allows the solution to be a co-operative rather than an antagonistic act.

Top tip 4: Mirror behaviour [1.3] [2.9] [3.3.2] [3.3.4]

Put yourself in the pupil role acting out using an overloud voice. For example: *Give me that pencil* (very loudly). They can then view the effect. This helps to bring about an attitude change as the pupil is faced with the other's viewpoint.

Deletions, distortions and generalisations

Bandler and Grinder (1975) have drawn attention to the way we limit our communication by a constant use of deletions, distortions and generalisations.

Deletions

Example: *When I take your group for literacy hour I get annoyed.*

What are you annoyed about and who causes the annoyance? We often miss elements out when we talk but it may not make our meaning clear for the pupil. *Tom, I am getting annoyed* is incomplete and unclear but *Tom, your pen tapping on the table distracts me*, makes it obvious what the problem is.

Distortions

Example: *My choice of Wednesday to work is difficult – Choosing Wednesday to work is difficult.*

Statements are often distorted by changing an ongoing process into a fixed event, using a noun instead of a verb. Changing the statement by using a dynamic verb instead of a static noun allows re-evaluation.

Generalisations

Example: *I find this group difficult.*

Are there no easy children? Generalisations like this are an explanation for not behaving in a certain way. It means blame is unfairly attributed. The statement: *Tom is always talking in class,* may mean Tom does not understand the lesson, or someone is constantly asking him for explanations. There are alternative ways of viewing this as the meaning is not clear.

We all use these limiting expressions but if we reduce them a little it would certainly help communication and interaction and improve discipline.

Questioning talk

Adults shoot questions at children in class as if they were firing on the enemy. Susskind (1979) estimated that teachers ask questions at the rate of two per minute whilst pupils ask at the rate of two per hour. Wragg (1993: 3) found that in 20 observed lessons there were less than 20 questions from pupils and these were procedural (*What time are we going home?*) rather than cognitive (*Why is the sky blue?*). A five-year-old returning from her first day at school announced that the teacher was no good because she *just kept asking us things*. At home it is the children who ask the questions whilst adults give the answers, so this was strange grown-up behaviour! Delamont (1976) suggested that cross-questioning, checking up and interrogation are rude in everyday life, but the staple of classrooms. Perls (1969) reminds us that questions often cover up implied statements and defend us against revealing feelings. For example: *Would you get out your books, please?* means *I want you to get out your books.* So why do adults use so many questions in school? Pate and Bremer (1967) suggest four reasons why and quantify their use.

To check knowledge	69%
To diagnose difficulties	54%
To recall facts	47%
To assist thinking	10%

Adult use of questions in school

Does it surprise you how little emphasis is given to helping children think? This is the basis of understanding – knowing something and being able to reflect about it in various ways. Knowledge is not the same as understanding. Although I know about human genomes and could answer many questions on them correctly, I do not understand how they work.

Question types

There are two question types and response patterns: a closed approach which suggests a response has been decided and an open approach which suggests a response that is a matter of choice.

Closed approach – suggests a response has been decided

Pupils are asked to:

- **Define:** define a word/concept with accuracy evaluated.
- **Describe:** describe an object, event, location with conciseness/accuracy evaluated.

- **Designate:** give a single word answer with correctness evaluated.
- **Displace:** manipulate information (calculation) with correctness evaluated.

Such questions place power entirely with the questioner and the only reward is if the answer is deemed correct. Pupils' hatred of questions is based on their familiarity with this format. They are unwilling to respond if they do not know the answer.

Open approach – suggests a response that is a matter of choice

Pupils are asked to:
- **State:** invited to give views, with the questioner encouraging and affirming with positive body language.
- **Evaluate:** offer opinions about the appropriateness of an action, situation or event with the questioner supporting with evidence.
- **Infer/predict:** make inferences from evidence and predict possibilities with the questioner facilitating justification of views.
- **Compare/contrast:** describe/explain similarities and differences between things with the questioner encouraging perceptions.

So, when do you employ the different question approaches? The closed approach is more suitable for what, which, who, where and when questions, as these tend to produce facts and specific information. The open approach, on the other hand, demands more explanation and is likely to involve a why/how question, generating ideas about feelings, motives and processes. Could/would questions ask the listener to explore their own potential.

Top tip 5: Question effectively [1.3] [2.9] [3.3.2] [3.3.4]

Understanding what type of question to ask each pupil is the key to successful responses. Use closed questions for pupils with limited thinking and language, and open questions to encourage narrative discourse.

Discourse (connected speech or writing)

Blank's (1985) levels of discourse suggest when open and closed questions can be used. She assesses the reasoning level required by a question and participant interactions. Four levels of discourse are described and have been extended (Sage, 2000b):

- matching here and now;
- selective analysis;
- re-ordering of perception;
- reasoning about perception.

The levels of difficulty determine the thinking and language structures that lead to understanding rather than frustration. We need to expose children to complex thinking and language for learning. Blank and Marquis (1987) suggest that adults must balance questions with comments. Questions require a response from

DISCOURSE LEVEL	QUESTION EXAMPLE
Matching what you see (immediate situation)	*What is this?*
Selecting aspects of what you see (immediate situation)	*What colour is the car?*
Re-ordering what you see (beyond immediate situation)	*Show me the cars that aren't red.*
Reasoning about what you see (expressing cause and effect)	*Why are you wearing a coat?*
Explaining a familiar experience (selecting possibilities that are not immediate)	*How do you cross the road?*
Imagining an unfamiliar situation (predicting possibilities that are not immediate)	*How would you spend a lottery win?*

Levels of difficulty

pupils. *Why are you wearing a coat?* (level 4). *You're wearing a coat because it is cold*, is a level 4 *comment,* exposing a pupil to more sophisticated thinking and language but avoiding a failing response. A level 3 *question* might be: *What do you wear when it is cold?* and a level 2: *What colour is your coat?* Problems stem from pupils being asked questions above their thinking and language ability. Although important in scaffolding children's thinking, framing and organising information, questions should be balanced by comments.

Dos and Don'ts of questioning

DOS – EFFECTIVE QUESTIONS	DON'TS – COMMON ERRORS
Extend and lift discussion to a higher level	Questions above the pupil's thinking and talking
Start with narrow focus (recall) and broaden (new ideas)	Too many questions and too few comments
Start with broad focus (outline) and narrow (detail)	Asking and answering a question yourself without giving the pupil time to think
Take a circular path – series of questions returning to initial idea	Asking questions of only the brightest, eager pupils
Take a straight path using similar questions	Asking the same type of questions repeatedly
Provide a backbone/scaffold for hanging ideas	Asking questions in a threatening manner
Use questions in balance with comments	Putting down pupil responses
Differentiate pupil discourse levels	Ignoring answer and repeating question to another
Signal that participation is valued and extend answers	Failure to correct an answer sensitively
Arouse and sustain interest in a topic	Failure to build and extend answers

Effective questioning

Some pupils could answer a narrowly focused question: *What's the name of the water droplets that fall from clouds?* requiring the answer *rain*, but be unable to cope with a broader one requiring an explanatory answer, such as *Why do we need rainfall?*

REFLECTION POINT 16 [1.1] [3.2.2] [3.3.1]

Here are some questions that probe and develop thinking. Which ones suit a high level of discourse ability and which ones suit a low one?

- Can you give me an example?

- Is that always the case or are there exceptions?

- What are the exceptions?

- How does that fit in with what we have said?

- Why do you think that is true?

- Are there any other views you can think of?

- What is the difference between the two?

- What are the similarities between the two?

- You say that it is y (for example, apples). What kind of y (apples) do you think we grow in England?

Explaining talk

Explaining something clearly to a pupil is the art of good teaching. As a teaching assistant you constantly have to explain things that pupils have not understood. The word 'explain' is used differently. Consider these scenarios:

- *Miss, can you explain what this word means?*
- *You have been told it is raining, which explains why you can't go out to play.*
- *Why are you hanging around the toilets? I want an explanation.*
- *Can you give me an explanation of what happens when you bake a cake?*

In the first situation, the adult is asked for the meaning of a word. In the second, the identification of a relationship between cause and effect is clarified. The third case asks for an explanation probably preceding a reprimand. Finally, the explanation could vary in complexity according to pupil age and understanding. The dictionary presents 'explaining' as giving understanding to another, allowing for its many contexts. Explanations help someone understand:

- concepts – including new ideas as well as the development of existing ones;
- cause and effect – the consequence of one thing on another;
- procedures – rules or requirements;

- processes – how things happen or work;
- purposes – why someone is doing something;
- relationships – between people, things or events.

Some explanations include all features. For example, in a Year 5 class about World War II, an explanation involved:

- concepts – aggression, defence;
- cause and effect – what led to the outbreak of hostilities;
- procedures and processes – the rules of war and how it was conducted;
- purposes – why it happened;
- relationships – Hitler and the Jews.

There are two parties: the 'explainer' and 'explainee'. It is often a reciprocal experience, with pupils explaining what they do not understand. This demands a certain level of thinking and expression to know what you know and what you don't. Adults working with children need to:

- find out what children know and understand about the topic;
- use words and phrases that are clear;
- discover misconceptions that need clarifying.

Explanations have three phases:

1. The overview/opening

This sets the scene and prepares for what follows. It is called an 'advance organiser', but there is a debate on how effective this is. Although evidence suggests children achieve better understanding and higher test scores if given 'advance organisers', it is argued that telling them what is going to happen spoils the mystery and reduces motivation. Miller's (1984) work on top-down and bottom-up processing is relevant, suggesting 50 per cent prefer bottom-up, deductive organising strategy, whereas the rest have a top-down, inductive approach. Those with the preferred top-down style need the overview before they can slot in the detail, whereas others with a bottom-up style process information in an on-going way. In Miller's (1984) puzzle (opposite), the bottom-up learners might find an animal's leg in one of the black portions, leading to a search for the rest of the animal. The top-down processor looks for a general outline of the figure.

Experience suggests that those with a top-down preferred strategy depend on advance organisers for effective processing of information whilst bottom-up ones are not so concerned about the overview. This knowledge demonstrates the complexity of teaching groups. There is evidence to suggest we learn best with teachers having the same preferred style of information processing as us. Can you recall teachers that suited you better than others? This is probably the reason!

From L Miller, in G P Wallach and K G Butler 1984
See Appendix 3 (page 137) for answer.

Such information is useful when planning approaches. Work by Smith (1998) highlights the issue of preferred mode of sensory processing with 24 per cent preferring information through words and 27 per cent through pictures and 37 per cent through hands-on learning. This suggests the wisdom of presenting information using words, pictures and real experience to take account of those who like to hear, see or involve themselves actively with information. Considering personal differences in learning style is important to successful teaching. Think of something you want to present to a child or children. How do you use words, pictures and active learning to transmit this information?

To sum up the overview, openings have several purposes to:

- preview what is to come;
- arouse curiosity;
- tune into individual learning styles through auditory, visual or experiential input;
- discover what children already know about the topic;
- refresh memories of previous learning before new material is introduced.

2. The on-view/exposition

Some explanations need a logical, linear approach as in a mathematics problem requiring adding and multiplying before finding the area of a playing field. Not all subjects follow this mode. Take history as an example. You could sequence World War ll in chronological order but also argue for a different approach. It might be better to review what pupils know and move back from present time to explain hostilities. Personal preferences are important and some favour a planned approach whilst others like to feel the group and use an intuitive approach in response to pupil needs. In any event, the middle part of an explanation will involve the selection of events. Confine information to three key themes to fit the memory limit. Too many headings and ideas mean that information goes in one ear and eye and out the other!

3. The review/ending and reflection

The final part of any explanation is important, bringing previous information together, re-stating it and stamping a personal view on the content. People remember what they hear first and last as the middle bit is when attention wanders! Make sure key ideas are stated clearly in the overview and repeated in the review. Some children suffer from a 'recency effect', when they only recall what they have just heard. These are pupils with limited ability to thread together events and produce a mental outline. They need help with comprehension strategies.

Top tip 6: Produce explanations that are understood [1.3] [3.2.2] [3.2.3]

Try using this plan to IMPRESS and produce explanations that are understood:

Idea – decide on key ideas

Method – structure points in a plan – use anecdotes as illustrations

Presentation – think about posture, voice pitch, power, pace, pause and pronunciation

Recipients – adjust information to receivers' level

Emphasis – review points at intervals to emphasise key ideas

Style – employ a formal/informal style that is appropriate for audience and situation

Safety – be safe and check listener understanding with questions

Analysing explanations

Let's take an explanation to analyse. For example, a lesson on pets.

- What precedes? (talk about pets)
- What happens? (pupils collect pictures and describe these in pairs)
- What results? (a collective poster about pets with written descriptions)
- What comparison can be made between views? (bar chart of pet preferences)

Taba (1966) believed that once adults knew how to analyse communicative processes they could move pupil's thinking to higher levels. We can apply this to the lesson on pets.

- Specific items of data (what animals are we going to learn about?)
- Comparing (what are the differences between dogs and cats?)
- Explanation (how do we look after pets?)
- Inferences (what happens if our pet becomes ill?)
- Logic (what happens if we forget to feed our pet?)
- Generalisation (can you think of other things or people that we need to look after?)

Stimulating children to think in different ways is important for the development of knowledge and understanding. Bloom's (1956) *Taxonomy of Educational Objectives* describes a six-level hierarchy, which is useful when differentiating pupils' work.

1. KNOWLEDGE – facts from observed/recalled situations
2. COMPREHENSION – understanding and interpreting
3. APPLICATION – using knowledge in different contexts
4. ANALYSIS – perceiving patterns and meanings
5. SYNTHESIS – combining, generalising and concluding
6. EVALUATION – assessing, verifying, reflecting

Those learning slowly benefit from activities targeted at levels 1 and 2, whereas able students are stimulated and extended by tasks that concentrate on application, analysis, synthesis and evaluation, allowing creativity to be fully harnessed.

Pupil explanations

Children need to share knowledge to clarify thinking and deepen understanding. Set up activities where a pupil has to explain to others (for example, a game). [3.1.3] Use criteria:

- clarity – is the explanation clear to others?
- language – is the verbal and non-verbal language relevant?
- structure – is the information organised?
- examples – are demonstrations or examples used to illustrate?
- learning – is something learned for 'explainer' and 'explainee'?

If pupils are encouraged in show and tell routines, their follow-on written tasks will be more fluent and organised. The thinking has been done, allowing concentration on presentation. Some students will never write well unless they have an oral-written approach. Nate Gage got to the root of explanations in his book:

> *Some people explain aptly, getting to the heart of the matter with just the right terminology, examples and organisation of ideas. Other explainers, on the contrary, get us and themselves all mixed up, use terms beyond our comprehension.*
>
> (Nate Gage, 1968: 47)

Non-verbal skills

> *An eye can threaten like a loaded and levelled gun; or can insult like hissing and kicking; or in its altered mood by beams of kindness, make the heart dance with joy.*
>
> (Ralph Waldo Emerson, 1860)

*Tom looks me in the eye and takes a deep breath. He then shrugs his
shoulders, presses his lips and looks anxious. I smile, look on with interest and
point to the book on his desk. It is Tom's homework.*

This incident demonstrates communication without words – a non-verbal
discussion about the late arrival of homework. We receive and make non-
verbal signals of facial expression, gesture and movement constantly but
seldom think about their significance or importance. Non-verbal signs reveal
feelings and attitudes more accurately than words. What signals do we send?

Appearance

How a person looks reveals much about their personality, role, job and status.
Extraverts dress in bright, unconventional garb. Solicitors in court wear
sombre suits in keeping with the mood of the occasion and are now told not to
wear pinstripes or polka dots as they are distracting (Law Solicitors
Guidelines). In school, a smart appearance shows authority. By dressing well
we show commitment and respect. Fortenberry (1978) says we are more likely
to obey people dressed in a high-status manner. Sage (2000b) suggests that
pupils value adults who are well dressed, and take pride in their appearance.

Body language

A listener relies more on the message contained in the speaker's body
language than on what is actually said, especially if the two contradict. Can
you recall saying a pupil's picture looked nice, when the grimace on your face
spoke otherwise? We lie with words but not gestures and are guilty
sometimes of a mismatch between what we say and do. There are two groups
of body language:

- kinesics (facial expressions, gestures and body movements);
- proxemics (touch, proximity, positioning, posture).

Kinesics
Facial expressions

Facial expressions are used in combination with speech. A listener provides a
continuous reaction to what is said by small movements of eyebrows and
mouth to indicate surprise, disagreement, pleasure or puzzlement. A speaker
accompanies utterances with relevant expressions that frame what is said,
showing whether these are funny, sad, serious or important.

The face communicates information in three time-scales: There is the
permanent face – we think of those with high foreheads as intelligent, thin
lips as prim and careful and protruding eyes as excitable. Such interpretations
may not be accurate. Secondly, the face expresses emotions that take time to
develop, as when muscle tension increases in anger with blood flowing to the
head and eyes bulging. Finally, the face flashes rapid signals to provide
feedback to others, such as smiles, frowns, nods and eyebrow movements.

Using facial expression to support ideas and provide feedback to others is vital. Note how poor communicators have little facial expression. Develop yours by reading poetry aloud, which practises performance skills.

Gesture

Primary school staff constantly use specific gestures to express the size, height and width of things they are describing. This is because relative words like big/small, tall/short, etc. are difficult for children to grasp, so gestures help to transmit meaning. Hand movements are most frequently employed but body ones co-ordinate speech and are known as 'baton' gestures because speakers gesticulate like band-leaders to keep their communication performance together.

Ekman and Friesen (1972) distinguish between hand gestures.

- **Emblems** directly translate into a word/phrase such as 'stop'. As meanings vary between cultures they may cause confusion in multicultural classrooms.
- **Illustrators** accompany speech with no specific meaning but to enhance the word as in a wide, round movement when talking about something circular. Some speakers 'flutter' their hands, and distract.
- **Adaptors** are self-oriented movements, such as scratching one's neck, and distract.

If you look at people in conversation they mirror each other's gestures, such as crossing arms or legs, and this imitation is important in establishing effective interaction.

Top tip 7: Use gestures to aid expression [3.2.2]

As a teaching assistant, you should use gestures to aid expression and emphasis but beware of movements that distract!

Proxemics
Touch

The British are one of the least touching nations, which produces problems when communicating with other cultures. Within broad social rules, touching helps us to get on better with others. When touched briefly on the arm, for example, we feel friendlier towards that person. Wheldell (1986) found that touch was an effective reinforcer of work and positive behaviour, when accompanied by praise. With present emphasis on child rights and accusations of physical abuse, some staff consider it expedient not to touch pupils under any circumstances.

Proximity

Everyone needs a certain space around them and feels threatened by too close a presence. Crowded classrooms and corridors are waiting for disruption to happen and pupils lash out if oppressed. The meaning of proximity varies between cultures. Arabs and Latin Americans stand close to each other, whereas the English, Scots and Swedes keep a further distance. Proximity signals the nature of relationships and we stand closer to those we like. It signals the boundaries that are required in situations and is a sign of attentiveness. Desks, grouped in a semi-circle rather than in rows, help adults keep proximity with students, as this encourages contact with the whole group rather than just the central band. This point is useful when trying to maintain attention.

Posture

Posture is the way we arrange our whole body. In practice, body posture merges with specific gestures and gives us away. If relaxed, others approach us confidently but if tense, with shoulders hunched, arms folded and fists clenched, people are wary. Look at these five stick figures. What do they suggest to you? [1.5] [3.2.2]

Body language (from Sage, R (2000b) *Class Talk* published by Network Educational Press)

Fenton (1973) says most pupils have such bad posture that they are permanently damaging their bodies. Posture may suggest inner turmoil. Someone with clenched hands and hunched body might be working through traumatic events in their mind. Encourage relaxed postures. Get pupils to practise sitting with feet firmly on the ground and hands on both knees to free up tension.

Paralanguage

Paralanguage comprises the non-verbal sounds accompanying speech. We may gasp with surprise, er and um, scream with fright, groan in pain or squeal with delight. The most important elements of paralanguage are the prosodics known as 'verbal dynamics' – the pitch, pace, pause, power and pronunciation that create the melody and meaning of words. I can shout *Tom* to show anger, or trill his name to indicate pleasure. The voice goes up and down musically as the diagram indicates:

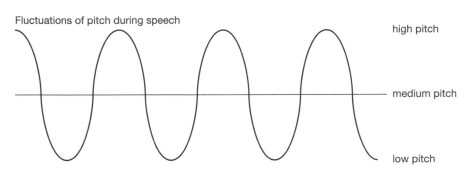

Fluctuation of pitch during speech (from Sage, R (2000b) *Class Talk* published by Network Educational Press)

According to Crystal (1971) intonation is the most important means we have of organising our speech into units of meaning. Think of the phrase: *Meet me in the staffroom at 3.30?* If performed with a rise at the end, a question is indicated, but a fall in voice pitch indicates a command statement. English is a stress-timed language, as every word of more than one syllable has one segment emphasised more than the others. Think of *communicate*. Where does the stress come? The power is on the second syllable.

Try varying meaning by shifting word stress:

1   2   3   4
Tom drank his milk
Stress on 1: Tom, and no-one else drank his milk.
Stress on 2: He drank it – he didn't throw it away.
Stress on 3: Tom didn't drink anyone else's milk – only his own.
Stress on 4: Tom drank milk, not orange or water.

Research into child language and learning difficulties (Sage, 1990b) indicates the problems pupils have in monitoring the verbal dynamics of speech. Introducing them to performance techniques in poetry and drama has a positive effect on their comprehension because they are helped to become aware of how meaning is made. Ability to use voice well is a major advantage in teaching children. Mehrabin (1972) shows that only seven per cent of the effective meaning is through the word, 38 per cent comes via tone of voice and 55 per cent from gesture. Thus, 93 per cent of the meaning is available from non-verbal channels. Few people are aware of this fact and as a culture we give little consideration to speech. In a teaching role it is vital to pay attention to what happens when we communicate. Good communication develops our confidence and ensures we receive positive feedback from others, which is the way we develop our self-concept and esteem. Eighty-five per cent of what we know is achieved by listening, but this is possible only if utterances are well formed and performed.

Tips for top talkers [2.9]

- Sip water and practise yawning for energy to speak and a relaxed approach.
- Check posture: keep feet 30 cm apart, weight balanced and slightly over toes.
- Relax the body by stretching up through your toes, feet, legs, hips, waist, chest, arms, neck and head. Pretend someone cuts the string holding your head up. Flop from your waist and slowly bring your body into standing.
- Check breathing: breathe in right down to the bottom of your lungs, pause and breathe out. Cup your rib cage at the bottom so you strengthen movements against resistance.
- Put bounce into your voice: count from your lowest possible note to the highest then reverse.
- Use the sentence: *I want a big, beautiful bouncy voice,* saying it sadly, happily, angrily, aggressively, excitedly and as if you were in a large hall.
- Take a piece of text and read it for different audiences: children, teenagers and older people.
- Visualise the moon. How do you convey its round, silvery, silent image with your voice? Lengthen the vowel and create movement by increasing and then decreasing sound.
- Take action words such as pull/push and as you mime the movement say the word.
- In a pair, listen to your partner telling a short story. Relay it back and change roles.

Support

Develop communication strategies and use them consistently to reap rewards in dealing with pupils effectively. Support, however, is needed to maintain and refine such activity. We need reinforcement from colleagues and parents, who can back up our actions, support our messages and provide appreciative feedback. Support produces contradictory reactions in our society. Some view this positively as it enables them to achieve things they might not do alone. Others feel that to admit support is needed displays weakness.

REFLECTION POINT 17 [1.4] [1.5] [1.6]

To explore your own attitudes, draw two support maps (see the examples below) to connect keywords and images – a positive and then a negative one – and show the people, groups, places, pets, objects and activities in your life that you experience as supportive/unsupportive. Then, try the following either alone or with a colleague. What words do you associate with support? Write a list and circle words that have a positive tone and underline negative ones. Pick two positive and two negative words and continue associations. For example, if you have written a positive word such as 'determination', you might list further associations such as 'strong', 'cope with set backs', 'confident in what I am doing', etc. If you perceive a word negatively you might list associations such as 'unfriendly', 'no time to give', etc. As you focus on links, you recall memories of experiences and find a pivot point between attitudes.

Postitive support map

Negative support map (from Sage, R (2000b) *Class Talk* published by Network Educational Press)

Look at the support map examples. On the one hand, support is enabling whilst on the other it can be limiting. Check your support maps. If you think that only weak people need support you may find your map rather meagre. If the reverse, your support need may prevent you from taking decisions alone.

Finally, review your current needs in school. List ways you would like support and how you might get it. What things are stopping you getting what you need? (Money for training?) How might you solve this? Do these activities if you want to improve your competences. From communication skills flow your ability to relate to others, organise and plan your own development. A checklist helps you on your way:

Check before you speak and act! [1.5] [3.1.3]

- Plan beforehand – have resources to hand and in order for tasks.
- Explore alternative views – look at what you say and do from others' perspectives.
- Check your work space – arrange seats so all see you and you can make easy contact.
- Eliminate interruptions/distractions, ensuring rules and routines are followed.
- Consider your audience – find out what interests them and makes them tick.
- Select an appropriate, comfortable style: firm, friendly but fairly formal if a lesson.
- Ensure verbal and non-verbal communication matches – get colleagues' feedback.
- Organise to time slot: let pupils pack away to involve them in disciplined routines.
- Relax and enjoy contacts with others and be prepared so you are calm and collected.
- Evaluate what went well and what could be better to develop your skills.

Talking with parents or carers

The communication abilities discussed in this chapter underpin all the activities we have to engage in when interacting with others. Successful people are successful communicators and the book *Class Talk* (Sage, 2000b) provides much more detail about this important aspect of personal and professional development. At this juncture, however, we need to bring out into the open issues regarding support staff talking with parents and carers. Some schools have clear policies regarding staff communication with carers. For example, it would not be acceptable for support staff to discuss some aspects of children's progress or lack of it, and guidelines would make this a responsibility of the Head, class teacher or in some cases the Special Needs Co-ordinator (SENCO). In any event, we all need to regularly review the basic principles framing our relationships with others. They are:

Confidentiality

We have to keep reminding ourselves of our responsibilities regarding sensitive information. Working in a school we become privy to many details about children and their parents. It is never acceptable to divulge personal information to others (even our living partners and family) in case it inadvertently falls into the wrong hands. It is wise to exercise restraint in revealing personal details about oneself or others and to refrain from any discussion of a pupil with another parent. It may seem patronising to mention this but we have to exercise vigilance and it is very easy to let something slip even when we intend not to. Trust your intuition and remain diplomatic and especially careful when parents attempt to quiz you about school situations or personnel. We have all had our comments misinterpreted and saying little avoids the possibility of this happening to a large extent.

Care

Support staff are often involved in difficult situations regarding children and it is vital to demonstrate care, co-operation, collaboration and a consistent approach in our dealings with others. Often when we are tired, off-colour or bowed down with our own problems, we reveal this in a lack of interest and enthusiasm in our manner and bearing. Professionals working in public institutions, such as a school, have to know how to become good actors, dismiss their own feelings and concentrate extra hard on others and their particular issues. *Comforting ability* has been shown to be one of the most important communication skills (Burleson, 1984, 1991). The value of support is clear when big problems arise but Ekenrode (1984) shows that small, daily distresses take the biggest toll on our mental and physical well-being. Providing a sympathetic listening ear is often all that is needed to cope with others' problems. Focusing on someone else's concerns broadens our understanding and suggests new ways to deal with issues, which then help us to decide what to think and do in similar encounters.

Clear messages

It is easy to assume that others share our understanding of the world and there is a general view that we are all knowledgeable about schools and education because of the long years spent there. However, there are constant changes operating in educational policy and practice that are not noticed unless one is actively involved. Values may be very different today from the school experiences of parents or carers. Never assume that children's carers understand what Standard Assessment Tasks, Legal Statements or League Tables are, or the nomenclature of staff such as SENCO or Director of Widening Participation. Parents often mention in research investigations that staff in school talk a jargon that they do not fully understand. Make an extra effort to explain things explicitly and check that listeners are making sense of what you say. It is patronising to question whether others understand you, but asking frequently if what you say is making sense is less threatening and important to check that the message is understood.

Summary

Support staff have a very important role in helping children access learning and develop appropriate behaviour within the complex situations in which they now have to operate. With inclusive policies now operating in schools, teaching assistants are essential to make them work effectively. Personal abilities to communicate, which involve a quick appreciation of what is required and the skill to respond appropriately in a range of situations, and with a variety of children and adults, demands a careful appraisal of our own strengths and weaknesses. This section has provided many points for reflection, and if we work hard at reviewing and refining our communication abilities we shall provide successful support and enable children to develop and flourish.

Teaching assistants need:

- to cope with a wide variety of tasks and relate closely to a range of people;
- to develop communication skills in one-to-one situations and with groups;
- to develop positive language and keep pupils motivated;
- to understand how to question pupils according to their particular levels of discourse;
- to understand the structure of explanations;
- to organise and plan activities within a time-slot;
- to evaluate their own skills and those of others.

4. Organising effective learning experiences

In the previous three chapters, we have thought about individual children's learning and looked at suggestions on how you can support it successfully. In this chapter we look more closely at the whole issue of organising effective learning for groups of children: in effect, the curriculum. Education is an experience that is founded in a body of knowledge of not only how children learn but how they should be organised for teaching. The chapter considers the meaning of 'curriculum'. It examines the decision processes that determine curriculum delivery and pattern and the principles that drive our practice, and offers the opportunity to explore some of the limitations of the National Curriculum.

Issues about education

We have looked at how children learn and reflected on the fact that they pick up knowledge and understanding in different ways and at differing rates. In a way, the idea of a genuinely child-centred culture is nonsense as young children must learn about the whole community they are born into and prepare for their place within it. Trends in society bring child and adult together but also force them apart. Longer periods of education are prolonging children's dependent status, but the intellectual gap between an educated adult and a child is now so large that only sophisticated learning systems can bridge this. The spread of higher education and increasing technical complexity of so much adult work has exaggerated the differences between child and adult worlds.

This has enormous implication for education, which has to address the needs of a society with complex, technical activities rapidly shifting away from heavy industry to a massive increase in people services. In its broader sense, education is about acquiring and using knowledge and developing our mental skills to understand. There is also the expectation that it can cure our social ills and compensate for poverty, abuse, and any other sort of personal difficulty a child may bring into school. The increasing status and importance of teacher assistants has resulted from the latter expectation, as the 1981 Education Act brought in legal statements to ensure support for children who have severe physical, mental, emotional and social difficulties. Teacher assistants are employed in schools not only to fulfil a general role in assisting the teacher in class but a specific one supporting statemented children with very complex needs. So what are the functions of education that have to be organised?

Academic skills

The traditional skills of reading, writing and arithmetic are essential to survive a modern world. As we seek to raise standards there are an increasing number of children who need support to achieve the expected key stages. The teacher assistant has a major role here. At the root of most basic skill difficulties is an inability to cope well with language and the teacher assistant is well placed to help pupils access learning by taking groups of children who need communication help. Cooper (2001) has reviewed schemes and recommends the Communication Opportunity Group Scheme (COGS) (Sage, 2000a), circle time (Moseley, 1996), and nurture groups (Boxall, 1996) as successful ways of helping children talk. COGS concentrates on developing thinking and communication in both spoken and written tasks whereas circle time and nurture groups are built on the idea of encouraging talk to develop self-esteem. Transferable key or core skills are part of the thinking of the development of an adaptable, flexible workforce of the 'skills economy', along with ICT. Thus communication as well as literacy and numeracy have been promoted up the agenda particularly within post-16 learning. This will become an increasing speciality for teacher assistants in schools.

Socialisation: social control and order

Socialisation is a process of induction into society's culture, norms and values. This ensures a level of social cohesion necessary for society to continue. School, along with the family, has a crucial role here. In order to live a safe and ordered life we must be aware of the expected ways to behave. These may be seen as norms of behaviour or manners. Think about how we behave in an orderly manner for much of our lives without thinking about it. We say 'please' and 'thank you' in appropriate circumstances and learn to queue for school meals or to get into class from the playground. In public places, like school corridors, we walk sensibly without bumping into others and touching people. We maintain appropriate distance and eye contact when talking with others. These norms are learned and TAs are vital in this process. Much of what they do is incidental to the academic tasks – reminding children not to talk while the teacher does, and not to push and shove whilst waiting for something. All through the school day, the TA is focusing on the children, pointing them in the direction of good social control and order whilst the teacher concentrates on the curriculum. Teaching assistants have, therefore, a major responsibility for organising a child's social learning.

Preparing for work

In small, self-sufficient societies, children learn survival from surrounding adults, who are multi-skilled and can satisfy most of their learning needs. In these contexts, the adult is a mentor unlike the teacher, who stands in front of a group and transmits knowledge. As forms of employment have diversified and become specialised, so specific training has been needed. Payment in the form of wages reflects the level, scarcity and importance of the skill required. The general qualities needed for employment, such as those expressed in the transferable skills, can be developed at all levels of education. Job-specific training is likely to be based in the workplace, but is likely to involve further and higher education. The role of preparing pupils for work is being increasingly seen as an important one for schools to focus on. It is ideal for TAs to specialise in as it involves personal coaching, the skill that they develop from their work with individual children.

How do these functions work together?

These functions of education may appear to overlap. Preparation for work involves personal skills such as communication, presentation and team-work as well as developing the mind and acquiring relevant knowledge. Socialisation and internalised social control are also a part of this. Different functions may be to the fore at various stages of a pupil's education. Whereas it is appropriate to stress the development of the mind, expression of thinking and individual freedom to explore and experiment at specific times, it is also important to stress the discipline and self-control needed to fit, not only into school, but also society.

Although all functions are appropriate, together they may cause tensions. For example, developing thinking and communication encourage a questioning attitude, but the need to maintain social order involves obedience and correct behaviour. This could be viewed as the development of accepting rather than questioning individuals. Teachers and teaching assistants encourage pupils to question issues to do with the topic studied. Much primary work is investigative and, with the emphasis on science and technology, children are constantly required to ask questions to do with electricity, friction, different materials, life cycles of plants and animals, etc. In other areas of school life, however, such as lesson choice, homework, discipline, uniform, tests, examinations, etc., there is no room for questioning, and children have to buckle down and conform. Obedience is a virtue, listed alongside independence and initiative, and employers also require it in large measure. A balance has to be struck between self-development and self-control, and the TA's function is supporting and encouraging students with this balance. This needs a clear understanding about human nature, the working of school, and the purposes of activities.

The emphasis placed on the different functions of education may be different according to the pupil's potential and performance level. Some pupils may be pushed academically because they are good at mental tasks; others will be encouraged in sport or practical skills because that is what they shine at. Davis and Moore (1967) saw this sifting of talent and allocation of individuals to appropriate roles in society as an important function of a formal education system.

Some argue that too much time is spent theorising about education, taking time away from the real issues. This assumes that there is agreement on what education is and how it should be conducted. Chris Woodhead (1999), then the Chief Inspector for Education, wrote in his annual report:

> We know what constitutes good teaching and we know what needs to be done to tackle weaknesses: we must strengthen subject knowledge, raise expectations, and hone the pedagogic skills upon which the craft of the classroom depends... Why, then, is so much time and energy wasted in research that complicates what ought to be straightforward?

This apparent rejection of alternatives could be viewed as an attempt to prevent debate and silence dissent. Research has been important, not only in understanding the child and how he learns best, but in pointing out the strengths and weaknesses of policies and practices. Education, because of its ideological base, will always be an important aspect of politics (Carr and Hartnett, 1996). It is a central and an increasingly important aspect of a complex, technological society. Education helps shape the future not only in the development of individuals but in the promotion of ideas. We all, as active participants in society, have our own views on education and how it should be organised. The interaction of competing interests renders it a stimulating and fascinating study.

REFLECTION POINT 18 [1.1] [1.6] [2.2] [2.3]

- Compile a list of what you think are the most important things a school should educate its pupils in. What is the basis for your views?
- Choose two learning experiences from your own education:
    - What was their impact on you?
    - How do they relate to your views on educating children?

A brief history of education

Elementary education

Systems of education evolved from the transformations of society that took place in the eighteenth and nineteenth centuries (Mann, 1979). Formally, education had been for only the rich, privileged section of the population. With the 'springing up' of large factories and the move from rural to urban communities, schools for the 'poor' became common. Children were drilled in a curriculum mainly concerned with teaching values, virtues, literacy, numeracy, hygiene, physical maintenance, domestic skills and basic knowledge about the world. Pioneers viewed education as the instrument of moral transformation necessary to survive the new urban communities. The first schools were for primary age children until they started work – much earlier than today. Secondary education only emerged after 1904 when new forms of transport were opening up possibilities in an increasingly mechanised and later technological world that demanded more sophisticated knowledge and skills.

The tripartite system

The end of the First World War signalled a shift in educational philosophy. *The Norwood Report* (1943) set out three aims for education:

- knowledge for its own sake;
- occupational knowledge and skills for industry, trade and commerce;
- practical studies to balance mind and body: humanities, sciences and arts (including sport).

The 1944 Educational Act is the defining moment in the history of education with a right for all pupils to a secondary education based on ability and aptitude with ordinary and advanced General Certificates in Education (GCEs) offered only to bright pupils.

a) Grammar schools with selection at 11 plus were for the academically able.

b) Technical schools were for the practically able to pursue careers like engineering.

c) Secondary modern schools were for those not fitting either of the above categories and provide a general education suitable for largely unskilled workers.

Comprehensive system

Criticisms about parity of esteem emerged and the selection procedures were increasingly discredited (Young, 1998). The move towards the comprehensive school was designed to heal the divisions, with schools taking all pupils within a geographical area and offering choice and diversity in the curriculum. There were different ways of organising teaching, with setting, streaming and mixed ability classes (from the 1970s). The GSEs were supplemented by a new form of assessment, the Certificate of Secondary Education (CSE), offering a more practical, flexible examination.

The National Curriculum

The 1988 Education Reform Act changed the nature of the curriculum and its authority. Previously each school had decided what it taught and when, and this had resulted in diverse standards across the country. The curriculum was now prescribed by law to ensure a consistent set of national standards. The National Curriculum was subject to frequent modifications in its early years but the current ministerial orders have been in place since 1995. Specific requirements concerning these subjects vary according to the ages of the pupils. In Chapter 1 you will have read, briefly, about the introduction of the National Curriculum, and recent curricular initiatives. The discussion centred around the changing roles of the TA and the impact that development of the curriculum had on those roles. It has been shown that having knowledge of what is taught and why it is taught should be considered crucial to effectiveness (HMI, 2002) but there are many issues surrounding the curriculum, and it would be impossible to cover all of them in depth, here. Instead it is hoped that you will be able to work though discussion of some issues, and activities, to build a review of the curriculum in your setting. In doing so you will be using some key skills for primary data collection which may give you practice when compiling future studies.

The Foundation Stage

In September 2000 a distinct curriculum for children aged 3–5 was introduced. There are six areas of learning each with a set of objectives referred to as Early Learning Goals:

- personal, social and emotional development;
- communication, language and literacy;
- mathematical development;
- knowledge and understanding of the world;
- physical development;
- creative development.

It is envisaged that most children will have achieved, and some will have exceeded these goals by the end of their reception year in school. In 2002 an Education Act extended the National Curriculum to include the Foundation Stage and the six areas of learning became statutory. More information can be found at **www.qca.org.uk**.

The curriculum

The word 'curriculum' refers to the course of study that learners follow, but can also cover any learning that goes on within school (Watkinson, 2002: 16). It is used in many contexts, and children can experience learning at many different levels. We are probably familiar with its use in specific contexts, such as when referring to the National Curriculum, for example. Some other ways of distinguishing between perceptions of curriculum were identified by Pollard and Tann (1994, in Hughes P, 2000: 22). These include the official or formal curriculum, the hidden curriculum, the observed curriculum and the experienced curriculum. Some aspects of the curriculum may be considered informal.

The formal curriculum

This is what most people are thinking of when they consider the curriculum. It is what you would expect to see written down. Your school has to deliver a programme of study, which includes the subjects that are legally required to be taught, and anything else that the school decides should be part of their programme. This will be recorded in the school's planning documents, and statements reflecting this should be conveyed in the prospectus. Schools have discretion to develop the whole curriculum to reflect their particular needs and circumstances. Considering the values that are appropriate for the school to communicate may be one determining factor; for instance, teachers at a small rural school wished to broaden the horizons of the children they taught, and included in their programme of study a partnership with a city multi-cultural school, and a visit to a mosque (QCA, 2002a: 8). Schools must have policies on behaviour and sex education, and many other aspects of school life. These may also affect the formal curriculum.

REFLECTION POINT **19** [2.2] [2.3] [3.1.4]

- Obtain a prospectus from your school, and analyse what is said about the curriculum. Are any 'extras' included or implied? Carry out this analysis by recording each statement about the content of what is taught in the left-hand side of a table. Then record whether each statement is an 'extra' in your opinion, or something that all schools should teach. You may want to return to this again before you finish this chapter to re-check your analysis against what you have learnt about the National Curriculum.

- If you find differences, is a rationale given for them?

- Can you suggest reasons, taking into account the circumstances of your school?

What is legally required?

Although there have been amendments, what is legally required to be taught in school is governed by The Education Reform Act 1988 and the Education Acts of 1997and 2002. These state that all state schools should:

Provide pupils with a curriculum that:

- *is balanced and broadly based;*

- *promotes their spiritual, moral, cultural, mental and physical development;*

- *prepares them for the opportunities, responsibilities and experiences of adult life;*

- *includes, in addition to the National Curriculum, religious education, and for secondary pupils, sex education.*

(QCA, 2002a: 6)

In England and Wales, all primary schools must teach religious education (RE), although documents are published separately from those of other subjects, as a locally agreed syllabus. They must also ensure that English and information and computer technology (ICT) are taught across the curriculum. PHSE (see below) including citizenship is also part of the National Curriculum. They must deliver the National Curriculum (NC) to all children from Year 1 onwards. The Foundation Stage now covers children in Reception classes, whether they have attained the age of five or not. From 2004 there will be a requirement for schools to be responsive to particular needs and to make learning more *personalised* (DfES, 2004). There is a statutory requirement to teach Information Communication Technology (ICT) across the curriculum, so that it supports learning in all subjects for KS2 and above, and at least the core subjects for KS1 and the Foundation Stage.

How the National Curriculum is organised

At primary level the subjects included in the National Curriculum are:

- art and design;
- design technology;
- English;
- geography;
- history;
- information and computer technology;
- mathematics;
- music;
- physical education, including personal, health and social education (PHSE);
- science;
- (Welsh).

The core subjects

In primary education the core curriculum consists of the subjects which all children have to learn, and which are central to their experience at school. These are English, mathematics and science. Many TAs will find that the subject matter of the core curriculum is central to their daily lives, too! As pointed out in Chapter 1, much of the teaching and learning involved in delivering English and maths is carried out during literacy hour and numeracy hour. However, the teaching involved in these strategies does not encompass all that is in the National Curriculum descriptions. A large part of the English curriculum is about spoken language development, and includes drama, for instance, whereas the literacy strategy focuses, particularly, on the development of reading and writing.

The foundation subjects

The foundation subjects consist of the rest of the list of subjects, which are required to be taught as part of the National Curriculum.

There is a programme of study for each subject arranged in key stages. In the primary sector these are:

Key Stage 1: covers Years 1 and 2, and level descriptors (more on these later) 1 to 3, with an expectation that the majority of children in Year 2 would reach level 2C in the core subjects.

Key Stage 2: covers Years 3 to 6, and level descriptors 2 to 5, with the expectation that the majority of children in Year 6 would reach level 4 in the core subjects (more on this later, too!).

Of course, even if you support learners mostly within one subject area, you will be aware that there is greater emphasis on some subjects than on others. Have you ever considered how such decisions are made? Although there are recommendations as to how long the teaching day, week and year should be, and how much of the timetable each subject should take up, schools are free to make such decisions for themselves, within the constraints of providing a broad and balanced curriculum. Most primary schools teach for an average of 22 hours a week (sometimes slightly less in Key Stage 1 and more in Key Stage 2).

REFLECTION POINT 20 [2.7] [3.1.1]

- Ask colleagues if they are aware of how time has been allocated to subjects, and why – maybe you can view some long-term planning documents for your school.

- Take a plan for a typical week of lessons appropriate to a class with which you are working. Analyse the time allocation for each subject in a similar fashion to the model below.

- Compare your results with the QCA recommendations.

SUBJECT	RECOMMENDED TIME ALLOCATION
English	24–36%
mathematics	18%
science	7%
art and design	4%
design technology	4%
geography	4%
history	4%
ICT	4%
music	4%
physical education, including personal, health and social education (PHSE)	6%
RE	5%
Total	84–96%

Recommended allocation of time per subject, QCA

There will be variations, of course. One reason will be because you are doing this for one sample week, and your school may have decided to deliver geography in a block of lessons, and might therefore, not be teaching history that week. This reflects the flexibility to organise the curriculum to suit the school.

The Dearing Report (1993) made some recommendations indicating that English should occupy 14 per cent, science 13 per cent, maths 12 per cent, technology, foreign languages, religious education and physical education 5 per cent each and the remaining 43 per cent should be discretionary but should include a balance of other specified subjects.

Related strategies

Information Communication Technology (ICT) across the curriculum

There is a considerable commitment to providing for the diverse and particular needs of children, and promoting the potential for all. ICT can provide the key to equal access for children who have limited ability in a particular area. For instance, working with a TA to word process work that others are hand-writing may provide a child who has poor manipulative skill with a chance to complete and be proud of work within the same time frame as the rest of the class. It is recognised that the use of ICT can help children take *greater responsibility for their own learning, plan and organise their ideas, and produce and present work of a high standard. It can also encourage creativity* (**www.nc.uk.net/ld/ICT_respond.html** July 2004).

Health and safety

Where children work with tools, in practical sessions (including ICT) and in different settings such as visits, it is expected that they will be made aware of hazards and risks involved. They should be taught to assess these, not just at the beginning of an activity, but as an on-going process, and be able to explain steps taken to ensure their health and safety (**www.nc.uk.net/nc_resources/html/health.shtml**).

Citizenship

At KS1 and 2 citizenship is part of the curriculum for PHSE. It appears as a separate subject at KS3 and beyond. For primary aged children the emphasis is on becoming mature and responsible members of the community, locally, nationally and internationally. Children are helped to appreciate and respect different ways of living, and to look after their environment. This is linked to the move towards *educational for sustainable development* – ensuring a better quality of life now and later. Objectives include appreciation of diversity, attention to the use of resources and thinking and carefully managing decisions about life and living conditions (**www.nc.uk.net/esd**).

Modern foreign languages

There is no requirement to teach a foreign language at KS1 or KS2, but the opportunity to do so from KS2 is recognised as providing a valuable experience educationally, socially and culturally. There are cross-curricular links, and the language learning can act as a medium for the reinforcement of other knowledge areas. Children are often fascinated by hearing and learning a different way to speak. There are non-statutory guidelines on the National Curriculum website.

The literacy and numeracy strategies

The National Curriculum is concerned with what is taught, and although it gives examples of how this is done it does not prescribe how teaching should be done. As a result of standards in National Tests being consistently lower than the Government was aiming for, the Literacy Strategy was piloted and then introduced into primary schools in 1998 (DfEE, 1998) and the Numeracy Strategy followed a year later (DfEE, 1999). Both strategies provide a model for structuring a daily lesson, beginning with a whole-class session, followed by a session of group or individual work and ending with a plenary session, which reinforces the main points of the lesson:

> In 1988 the first version of the NC specified the content of what should be taught in schools in some detail, but, it can be argued, in a way that asked teachers to select and interpret... In both (NLNN) strategies, government has prescribed pedagogy as well as content.
>
> (Hancock and Mansfield, in Collins et al. 2001: 97)

As with any new system, when the strategies were first introduced, teachers followed the models quite strictly and the system was seen as restrictive, repressing creativity for instance, but in visiting schools regularly I have seen that patterns of delivery have relaxed. In selecting texts, for example, teachers can make the most of cross-curricular opportunities, linking reading material with the focus of a programme of study from another subject. In one classroom, a teacher of a Year 2 class used a book on Victorian toys in the literacy hour, and design technology lessons focused on making a similar toy. Similarly the Katie Morag stories (Hedderwick, 1986) have been used to link literacy with geography. Modes of delivery have also relaxed – sometimes the plenary is being left out, for instance – though it is my belief that a lesson will lose some of its effect without it.

REFLECTION POINT 21 [2.1] [2.2] [3.2.3]

- Observe a literacy 'hour' (the recommended timing varies depending on the age of the children) or a daily maths lesson. Record the timings of each section of the lesson, and the activities that the children are involved in.

- Compare this lesson to the model provided in the National Strategy handbook. Were there any differences? If you have worked within this curriculum area for a while, or alongside different teachers you may well have further observations to make.

In order to measure whether progress has been made the Government sets targets; for instance, in literacy that 80 per cent of children in Year 6 would reach level four in the National Tests by 2002. At the time of writing it has just been revealed that this target has not been achieved, but of course, it will be 2004 before children who have experienced the Literacy Strategy throughout their schooling are tested. Many of the TAs I work with went to school at a time when grammar was not taught specifically, and the approach to reading did not emphasise phonic strategies, or use top-down and bottom-up strategies for coping with text. They report that they can see the difference in the quality of knowledge that children have due to the present system. The situation is similar in numeracy, where the emphasis on reasoning rather than learning algorithms (methods) will, it is hoped, make a difference. No system is perfect, however, and the QCA is constantly monitoring progress through the School Sampling Project, details of which can be viewed on the QCA website (**www.qca.org.uk**). Catch-up programmes such as the Additional Literacy Strategy (ALS) and Springboard5 have been so well received that they have been extended to older and younger children. All of these programmes rely on the use of additional adults to support teachers in the classroom. The presence of a TA has been shown to *have the potential to improve the overall quality of teaching* (HMI 2002: 30). Some aspects of support programmes are very often entirely delivered by teaching assistants.

REFLECTION POINT 22 [2.1] [3.1.2]

- Does your school use any programmes, which augment the Literacy Strategy or the Numeracy Strategy? What is the involvement of TAs in your school in these programmes? Do they have responsibility for organising any teaching sessions?

- Formulate a questionnaire that you can ask colleagues to fill in, or use as a basis for interviewing other TAs. Use these questions or similar ones. Compare findings when your survey is complete and try to make some statements as a result.

The observed curriculum

The observed curriculum is *what is actually taking place in the classroom, the lessons, the activities you see* (Hughes, 2000: 24). This is why I suggested you collected a plan to accompany the observation you carried out for the last section. What you actually see happening may be somewhat different from what was intended in the official or formal curriculum – the lesson plan. This could be for a number of reasons: experienced teachers sometimes make changes as they respond to the needs of the children, but would be sure of the educational reasons for doing so, and unexpected events sometimes encroach on plans.

REFLECTION POINT 23 [2.3] [3.2.1]

- Look back at the observation you carried out for reflection point 21. Compare what actually happened, using your recording, with the contents of the relevant short-term plan for that lesson:
  - What differences could you identify?
  - Did these detract from the lesson, or enhance it?

The experienced curriculum

What the children actually take away from the lesson may not be the same as the teacher intended in the official version of a lesson. If, for instance, a child has not understood part of a lesson, or not had a turn at an activity on offer, then the curriculum as experienced will differ from that planned. Teachers and TAs should have an awareness of this – being able to assess what the children have experienced is part of the assessment process, which will inform future lesson planning. The experience of the curriculum for some children can feel negative. If you think of what we know about Gardener's theory of learning – that people have multiple intelligences and their strengths in each of these varies – then the present primary curriculum, which leans towards academic achievement, will not suit everyone. Sharon, whom you will read about later, was able to address this in a creative way.

The informal curriculum

The informal curriculum can be viewed as not a legal requirement, and not necessarily formally recorded. This could include:

- learning opportunities offered through participation in school clubs, and teams;
- conventions to do with organisation, e.g. what happens at wet playtime, or how children are seated at assembly time;
- rules to do with access to areas of the school;
- standards concerning the appearance of the school and classroom, and the children.

Some such information may be written in policies, such as the behaviour policy, and others dealing with the environment of the school. As a member of staff it is important that you know what these policies are and adhere to the contents to support the school in giving a message of continuity to the children, and parents. You may be involved in informal provision of extra learning opportunities, or aware of practice, which is accepted, but not part of the official curriculum.

REFLECTION POINT 24 [3.1.4]

- Log one example for each of the bullet points above that is not part of the official curriculum in your setting.
- How do you think this provision contributes to the ethos of your school?
- Does your school make provision for children with artistic, musical or sporting abilities, for example, to develop their talents?

The hidden curriculum

The hidden curriculum encompasses learning that children 'imbibe', perhaps as a consequence of the organisation of learning experiences, or the values of the people teaching them. Aspects of the hidden curriculum could be positive. For instance; children receive the message that boys and girls are treated equally and offered the same opportunity to access resources such as the computer. Or they might understand that they are successful learners because they receive encouragement and acknowledgement of their efforts through rewards systems. Mostly, however, the hidden curriculum is seen in negative terms: *many schools have good personal and social education programmes, which acknowledge the **pervasiveness** (my emphasis) of the hidden curriculum and its influence on children's progress and attainment* (Hughes, 2000: 23). If the whole curriculum is to provide for children's personal, spiritual, moral, social and cultural development then all adults in schools must be involved in:

● providing for equal opportunities;

● promoting independence;

● promoting self-motivation;

● providing an atmosphere where everyone is made to feel valued, and responsible attitudes are encouraged.

REFLECTION POINT 25 [1.3] [3.3.3]

● Carry out an observation during a main teaching session in one class. Were there any examples of messages given to children about their work through:

  – organisation – are particular children always seen first, do certain groups have higher status?

  – attitude – 'boys line up first'?

● What values do you hold, personally, as regards education? How do these affect the way you work?

● Read the 'mission statement' or statement of values in your school's prospectus. Are there similarities?

Planning the curriculum

> **Sharon's story**
>
> *I am a TA in a large junior school which streams for most of its teaching. For some time I have been responsible for planning and delivering technology lessons to groups of about ten pupils at a time, and I know I'm fortunate to have my own teaching base for this. Late in the summer term I asked to be able to arrange some art lessons especially for children who had shown particular flair over the year, as part of our response to the needs of gifted and talented children. A particular group included a girl who is very dyslexic, and therefore has learning problems in most of her academic lessons. She knows that she finds schoolwork difficult. This group was a selection of children drawn from several classes of differing abilities. Suddenly she was working with children she knew were successful, and 'holding her own'. Being praised for her beautiful art work in a successful environment gave her some pride, and self-belief, and the renewed confidence she found enabled her to tackle other difficult areas with new determination. Everyone is good at something – we should make a real effort to find peoples' strengths, but sometimes it is hard to do this in school. I really want to carry out a project like this again when I can.*

Many teaching assistants are now involved in planning aspects of children's work, either alone or in partnership with other staff, though not many have the autonomy or the creative support that Sharon has. There are still a substantial number of school support staff who never see plans, and are not aware of how they work. It is important to realise that planning usually happens on three levels:

- Long-term planning – commonly for one academic year, under subject headings. Schools develop schemes of work, which show how they will deliver the National Curriculum subjects and other parts of the curriculum. Some may have rolling programmes in place.
- Medium-term planning – usually termly or half-termly and showing in detail what will be taught over this period. For literacy and numeracy the Strategy documentation (programmes of study for particular year groups and terms) may form part of this planning.
- Short-term planning – what happens weekly or, perhaps, daily.

If you do have access to plans, it is likely to be the short-term planning, which should show how additional adults in the classroom would be used. I phrase this thus, because parent helpers or other professionals may be included. Some class teacher's display plans or provide their TAs with copies in advance of lessons so that they are prepared for the content. This has the advantage that if a TA is supporting children with particular needs it is possible to adapt resources or differentiate activities in good time. An example of good practice I saw recently was during a lesson when the class were asked to cut up a sheet containing statements that had to be matched together, to assess whether they had absorbed key teaching points. Having had the lesson material in advance, the TA had adapted the sheet for her learner and incorporated colour coding to facilitate the matching. Another TA adapted class materials for use on the computer so that a child with physical special needs could access the lesson on an equal footing with his peers. Having a good relationship with the teachers you work with is essential, of course, since they should be able to trust your ability and use your strengths. You need to make sure you are informed, and ask if there are areas which you are not sure about.

Remember:

The quality of teaching is improved when the teaching assistant:

- *works in close partnership with a teacher who understands and plans well for the teaching assistant's role in the lesson;*

- *is clear about what she is expected to do, including how to give feedback on pupils' learning and behaviour.*

(HMI, 2002: 47)

The purpose of planning is to ensure that children are receiving the right kind of information in an appropriate format for their needs. Knowing the objectives of a lesson, and having targets for learning is essential to success. Targets should be SMART (Hughes, 2000: 69): **S**pecific; **M**easurable; **A**chievable; **R**ealistic and **T**ime-related.

So if you are preparing activities for children, try to make sure that you have a specific goal in mind that you think your child can achieve, realistically, within a given time. Also consider how the child is going to prove the target has been met – how you can measure the success. Hughes (ibid: 32) makes the point that measuring the success of objectives, which include words like 'enjoy' and 'understand', is very difficult. Choosing appropriate targets depends on working closely from appropriate plans – such as a child's IEP – and responding to assessment, one of the main purposes of which is to inform planning.

All planning should include the assessment of risk, and staff are responsible for keeping themselves safe as well as the children. As schools are accountable there should be a way of keeping track of decisions and research by means of an audit trail. In 2001 all schools were sent the government published document *Health and Safety: Responsibilities and Powers* which gives a great deal of helpful advice for planning activities in school and for out-of-school visits.

....

REFLECTION POINT 26 [3.1.1] [3.3.8]
_____

- Collect at least one example of long, medium and short-term plans used
  recently in your school. Make links, perhaps using a highlighter, showing where
  objectives in the long-term plans are further explained in the medium-term
  plans, and appear as specific teaching in the short-term plan. Show where any
  risk assessment has taken place and what the implications of the resulting
  decisions might have been.

- Were there any surprises for you?

- Are you involved in planning, or consulted in any way? At which stage?

....

Assessment in the curriculum

The National Curriculum is shaped by its assessment procedures. Gipps and
Stobart (1993) have described this as the assessment tail wagging the curriculum
dog! The framework was established as a result of the work of the Task Group on
Assessment and Testing, chaired by Paul Black (DES, 1989). It represented a major
break with past tradition and ownership, by establishing national, externally
marked tests known as the Standard Assessment Tests (SATs) at age seven, 11 and
14. The programmes of study for each subject are in booklets published by both
the English and Welsh Education Departments. Each subject divides into different
attainment targets. The ones for the core subjects are shown below:

ENGLISH	MATHEMATICS	SCIENCE
Speaking and listening	Using and applying mathematics	Experimental and investigative science
Reading	Number	Life processes and living things
Writing	Shape, space, measures and handling data (KS 2-4)	Materials and their properties
	Algebra (KS 3-4)	Physical processes

Attainment targets

In the Foundation Stage, baseline assessment schemes were replaced by a
single national assessment system – the Foundation Stage Profile – introduced
into schools in 2002–3. Each child in a government-funded place of education
must be assessed against thirteen scales pertaining to the six areas of learning.
These processes above are, of course, formal, statutory assessments.

As TAs you will be assessing all the time. Much of this happens informally, when
you weigh up whether a child will be able to carry out what is required by a task,
and then, perhaps, you modify it. You are assessing when you decide a child has
not understood and you re-present information, by re-phrasing, or using different
vocabulary, or fetching aids with which to explain a concept further. When you

feed back information regarding the lesson to a colleague this is the result of assessment. Feedback can also be done in the form of marking. In practice, some TAs mark children's work, and others feed back verbally to a child, and the teacher does any recording of marking. Your school is likely to have a marking policy as part of the assessment policy, which all staff should be aware of, but sometimes practice in marking is part of the informal curriculum – part of school life but not officially recorded. Ensuring you contribute to continuity by adopting agreed practice when feeding back to children is very important. Marking and feedback should focus on the positive, and the constructive; *criticism without guidance is not helpful* (QCA, 2000: 11). It is important to say exactly what you are praising or recommending needs improvement. Referring back to the objectives for a piece of work can help to do this usefully. *This is a lovely story* is complimentary, but *You have written a story with a clear beginning, middle and ending, just as you were asked to* is far more specific about the success involved!

Care should also be taken to appreciate the efforts and opinions of the pupil. Comments such as *try harder* can be demoralising if the child's perception of effort involved in a piece of work differs from yours (ibid: 11). In general, feedback should be about particular qualities of work, with advice as to what to do to improve, and should avoid comparison with other pupils (Black and Wilson, 1998, in QCA, 2000: 9). It is probably enough for most children to focus on no more than three aspects of a particular piece of work.

You are also likely to participate in formal assessment of children, since testing has become a feature of education today.

> However much it is argued that assessment should be curriculum-driven, it seems almost inevitable that, even at the most straightforward level ... 'teaching for the test' will happen – that the curriculum is assessment driven.
> (Ross, 2001: 126).

With the emphasis on raising achievement, and the requirement to meet targets set, it is impossible for those designing the primary curriculum to avoid being driven by the needs of formal assessment. Attainment targets form the basis for National Testing (SATs) at the end of Key Stages 1 and 2 in the primary sector.

Formal assessment can be:

- formative: celebrating positive achievements, e.g. in a record of achievement, where examples of 'best work' and interest are collected for an individual child;
- summative: where measures of what has been achieved over a given period of time are made at a specific point in time, e.g. National Tests (SATs) or end-of-term tests;
- diagnostic: to identify specific problems which may be addressed by appropriate use of teaching and learning strategies, e.g. analysing misconceptions in maths by studying the working out of a child and asking them to explain their thinking;

- evaluative: to determine the overall success of a particular initiative, for instance.

REFLECTION POINT **27** [2.2] [3.2.1] [3.2.4]

- Make a list of the formal assessments carried out in your school. Are you surprised at the range of tests there are? Most people would agree that children seem to be tested far too much, especially when presented with such a list!

- Identify one example of assessment with which you have been involved recently. Analyse the purpose of this assessment in terms of the points above. How did you record results so that they could be used constructively? How will this assessment inform planning? How did you feed back to the child?

Knowledge of the curriculum

Much has been said elsewhere about ways to support learning, in general terms. Although it is beyond the remit of this chapter to go into specific subject knowledge for each curriculum subject there are some points worth making.

Key topics

Each subject area has key topics, which are covered at specific times. I know this, but had it brought home to me anew last year when I visited Year 2 classrooms in schools across a wide area of Leicestershire and Staffordshire. Over a period of about three weeks I saw very many maps of the Isle of Strathay (Hedderwick, 1986). Most classes were making stick or finger puppets and writing dialogue for their own version of a well-known story – *The Three Little Pigs* and *The Billy Goats Gruff* figured largely! I could be reasonably sure that an objective for that term in geography was learning about geographical features such as island, sea, and coast. In English they would be focusing on grammatical features such as speech marks, and using speech bubbles to help show the difference between text and dialogue within it. In technology they were perhaps focused on joining materials together, and making parts the right size for the purpose, e.g. to fit on a finger. Sometimes schools may capitalise on the opportunity to work in a cross-curricular way by introducing topic work in the afternoon, which is planned to encompass the key concepts from several subjects. There are those (see for example, Hargreaves 1994 and Ryan, 1994: 194) who still believe that delivering the curriculum in separate subjects does not serve the needs of the 'whole' child.

However learning is arranged, making sure you are informed of the programme of study for a particular subject will help you feel more confident in supporting the children in their work. You can do this by reading the National Curriculum descriptions for the key stage that you are working with, and by reading the schemes of work within your school, but especially by being aware of the medium-term planning and the objectives for teaching each lesson.

Vocabulary and key concepts

Possibly even more useful is being familiar with the vocabulary and the key concepts that the children will meet in each subject area. For maths, for instance, there is an excellent vocabulary list for each year group included with the numeracy documentation. Knowing that the word 'half' and the concept of half is explored in the Foundation Stage and Year 1, means that you can take the opportunity to underpin the understanding by using the term and explaining it in other curriculum areas, or in social situations. People need to hear new words several times and in different contexts before they can use them, themselves, with confidence.

An important concept in the curriculum for history in Key Stage 1 is the idea of sequencing events chronologically (DfEE, 1999a). Sequencing events is also central to story writing and therefore part of the curriculum for English, and an essential skill when reporting for scientific experiments. Being aware of ideas and vocabulary that are common to education in general at particular stages will allow you to support and extend learning across the curriculum.

Resources

Usually TAs have a very good idea of the resources available in schools – you may well be responsible for keeping them in good order, or producing them in the first place! It is important to know how resources can be used to support learning in particular subject areas...and to see the potential for extending use to other areas. Individual white boards (which can be made by laminating a sheet of card) would be useful in any curriculum area. If you are aware that a child you work with is a visual learner you can provide opportunities to work with a variety of materials to help that child 'see'. Children who are operating at a lower cognitive level than their peers may still need the support of concrete materials in numeracy, for example. For older children it may be necessary to find resources that they don't mind using. A TA used tazos – small round discs with holographic pictures of cartoon characters on them, which many children were collecting – as a counting resource so that a child she worked with would not lose his 'cred' with his peers.

Strategies

Knowing what will be taught is important, but so is knowing how a subject is taught. Some subjects employ strategies for teaching, which you can reinforce. In literacy, for example, writing is scaffolded, so the children are given ideas and vocabulary on which to base each stage of a story or poem in a writing exercise. Watch out for examples of this – you will be able to use similar techniques when working with individuals or small groups, and in other subject areas too.

Letting children 'see' you thinking by speaking your thoughts out loud and modelling how thought processes could be followed through is extremely useful in maths, for instance. We want children to be able to explain their thinking, but for some children this will be very difficult indeed, so modelling how you do this may help.

Some subjects have subject-specific techniques and strategies. In numeracy lessons children are taught 'chunking' and 'bridging' in order to calculate mentally. When teaching reading you might encourage children to use their knowledge of onset and rime or to read to the end of a sentence to identify an unfamiliar word.

REFLECTION POINT 28 [1.6] [2.1]

- Choose a subject you support. Make a list of terminology you use or have heard used in the last few weeks, or half term.
  - Do you understand these words and the ideas behind them fully?
  - If there are any that you are not sure of, try to engage a colleague in discussion and improve your understanding...and therefore your effectiveness with the children!

Criticisms of the National Curriculum

Although many educationalists agree with the principles of the National Curriculum they deplore its installation and development (Lawton, 1999). Complaints relate to an absence of clear educational purpose, a disregard for learning development, and a failure to consult with teachers and other education professionals. Cajkler and Hislam (2002), for example, provide evidence to show how grammar has been misconceived and misapplied in the National Curriculum. Cajkler (1999, 2002) demonstrates the muddles and confusions emanating from government literature and says *there are now so many documents that it is not easy to find time to analyse, piece together and use them in an informed way* (2002: 163).

Most seriously, the National Curriculum accentuates class differences. The introduction of standard age-related tests means that children are ranked and ordered as never before and their value to school and workplace will vary accordingly. Children are differentiated against fixed norms, which provide powerful controls. The publishing of test results in league tables has led to the differentiation of pupil groups. They can become segregated from one another in bands or streams and follow different educational paths and social destinies. This works against equality of opportunity but sits well with the present system of grammar schools, comprehensives, city technology colleges, foundation and independent schools (Lawton, 1999).

The fact that children have differing abilities and interests logically presupposes that they need different learning experiences. Diversity has to be preserved and valued for a successful society. What seems to be at fault is the notion that academic education is best for all. The push to send 50 per cent of our children into universities denies the importance of technical, practical or general life skills. We need fewer thinkers and more doers to keep the world going and must cultivate attitudes that value practical careers. Recently, I went to hospital in the middle of the night with a very sick mother. I was in accident and emergency for five hours while she was being assessed. It was the cleaner who chatted, made tea and gave support. His role in hospital services was vital and yet medical professionals conveyed their superiority in the way they dealt with him. As long as we put academic knowledge on a pedestal, other forms of knowledge, such as knowing how to care for someone, will never be seen as equally important.

REFLECTION POINT 29 [1.6] [2.4]

- Visit the DfES website (**www.dfes.gov.uk**) and look up publications on educational developments. Read through some to identify key areas of education policy and practice. How do these ideas match your own thinking on the subject?

Putting ideas into practice

The impact of different ideas and beliefs is seen in what we teach children. However, knowledge can be structured and presented in different ways. Traditional subjects may be seen as important or knowledge can be presented in themes to reflect current affairs. For example, the theme: *How people live*, can include all subject areas and be organised for any age or ability group.

Learning and teaching can take many forms depending on the purpose of the curriculum and the skills and beliefs of teachers and teacher assistants. The emphasis may be on practical applications, experimentation, direct teaching, or open learning, where the child has materials to work through alone. A mixture of methods is often applied but we all have our favourite style that reflects our own preferences. As a teaching assistant you often work across classes and observe that pupils have very different experiences according to a teacher's own learning and communication style. One teacher may emphasise an interactive, oral approach whereas another targets writing and rote learning. The teaching assistant has to understand what and why these variations occur and be flexible and fit in with the particular organising style of the class in which she/he works.

Organising group learning

The teaching assistant is more concerned with knowing individual children well whilst the teacher targets the subjects of the curriculum. Their roles should be considered as complementary and equal in importance but with a different emphasis in their own education and training. Teachers develop subject knowledge and learn how to transmit it, whereas TAs acquire therapeutic skills that help children learn. These skills have been discussed in earlier chapters.

Teaching assistants have usually worked with individuals or small groups, and as the emphasis from 2004 (see Appendix 2) will be on tailoring education to suit needs wherever possible this will increasingly become their remit, under the guidance of a teacher. Understanding the dynamics of groups could make all the difference, providing the basis of successful learning. Individuals in a small group communicate face-to-face but the participants exercise a special influence on everybody's behaviour. Many studies (Gill and Adams, 1989) have looked at what makes groups work. There has to be a goal, and once everyone understands this, there is a process of 'storming', 'norming' and 'performing': storming is the settling in period when participants reveal their differences and personalities; some may be overbearing and even disruptive. Norming is the establishing of rules and how the group will operate and behave. Performing happens when the structure of operations is decided and can start. Each time a group convenes this process occurs. The two initial phrases are accelerated in an established group but need acknowledging in a warm-up activity to get children relating to one another and to remind them of the rules of operation. Studies have shown that groups without a leader have very unequal participation in which the active ones make the decisions and the passive ones agree. If you leave children to work on their own you need to discuss their roles and observe:

● behaviour that helps complete the task;

● behaviour that strengthens the group and values contributions;

● behaviour that disrupts the group's work.

Of interest to teaching assistants is the difference between a led group (wheel) and a non-led one (circle). The table below clarifies differences.

	LED GROUP (WHEEL)	NON-LED GROUP (CIRCLE)
Direction	Control centred on one person leading to a tendency to one-to-one communication.	No one in control and two-way communication occurs because more channels are available.
Speed	Group reaches decisions quickly.	Group take longer to reach decisions because there is more participation.
Accuracy	More likely to be inaccurate because there is less feedback. There is less danger of irrelevant issues interfering with the task.	More contributions giving more information and chance to correct errors. There is scope for digressions and irrelevancies.
Morale	Less involvement on the part of most members leads to lower morale.	Higher participation by everyone brings higher group morale.

Differences between a led group and a non-led group

The overall conclusions of research suggest:

- the one who handles the most information has the most status in the group;
- people like to set up routines/procedures and keep to them;
- people enjoy working in groups where they have most participation.

Sage (2000b) looks at the variety of groups a child might find himself part of, within a school day, and plots the most facilitating and the most inhibiting ones for a child who has a learning difficulty, using three-minute transcriptions of his performances. It is important to observe the groups in which children work best and to check that in a group children have a chance to participate. The research has looked at this aspect, and one of the aims of the Communication Opportunity Group Scheme is to teach children group skills so that they can learn effectively (Sage, 2000a). Some children do not have the communication skills to cope with a group, and pair situations are the best chance of developing these as long as the partners remain equal and the less able one is not dominated. Teaching assistants often work with children as a pair and have to check they don't do all the talking and allow the pupil to have control. It is worth noting that Lees et al (2001) have found that 73 per cent of children entering school have language and communication difficulties that interfere with learning. It is easy to dominate such children and do all the talking for them.

Summary

Education is an extremely complex business in today's society. The idea of globalisation, for instance, impacts on how we think about the relationships between culture, identity, institutions and practices. Post-colonial migrations have brought us a rich multicultural society in which communities with different value systems, forms of identity and social practices may live side by side with one another, mingle, mix and interact. Education plays a vital role in providing opportunities, experiences and structures for a range of cultural identities to find positive expression. Today's world no longer has fixed bearings, and traditional explanations no longer apply, because cultural intermingling is the order of the day.

In this shifting, uncertain and unstable world, education has to operate and manage knowledge, culture, conduct and values. Failure to engage positively with the diversity that children bring into school results in damaging inequalities. Although many problems remain in implementing an inclusive education policy, progress has been made. One of the important new forces in making this work is the teaching assistant, offering a fresh perspective to school practice and providing therapeutic experience for the increasing number of children who need extra learning support. The teaching assistant is an emerging professional, which with degree level qualifications offers real knowledge and expertise in today's school system.

You should, now, have built up a picture of how the curriculum works in your school...how the legal requirements, and the local 'flavour' of the community are brought together to create a programme of study which answers the needs of the children your school provides for. You should also have been able to extend your own knowledge of the curriculum, and have identified any areas which you may need to look into in more depth.

Some of the main points made are:

- education has evolved from an elitist to an inclusive system aiming to provide equal opportunities for all;
- anxieties have been expressed regarding the National Curriculum as it ranks children in a public way to an extent that it has never done before and this may affect children's life chances;
- education has a remit to develop not only academic but social and life skills to prepare children for jobs and participation in their communities;
- our multicultural society ensures that children not only have diverse abilities and interests but very different backgrounds and values which education has to merge and manage;
- teaching assistants play a major role in developing inclusive schools by providing therapeutic support for a large range of diverse needs.

You will have used techniques such as:
- observation, gaining an idea of what goes on by seeing children in action;
- surveys, finding out what goes on by asking people directly;
- interviews;
- analysing sources available to you, e.g. the school prospectus.

You should have enriched your understanding of learning in primary schools, of what children do, how learning is organised and how to support it effectively.

5. Developing your own learning

Overview

This chapter will help you:

- assess your own skills as a learner, in order to be able to appreciate strengths and identify areas that would benefit from improvement;
- assess your own learning style;
- prepare for study, considering various aspects of organising for learning;
- prepare for writing, especially for coursework, but also, perhaps, for writing in a professional capacity;
- explore reading, note taking and recording.

Many TAs now are taking courses, perhaps to advance their standing or career prospects, or perhaps to feel more effective in their role. Sometimes TAs are accorded more responsibility, or the focus of their role changes and they have to absorb new information to carry on. Being as well informed as you can be, though, requires the use of skills that may be 'rusty', or that you may not have developed as well as you might have liked previously. This section will consider some of these skills, giving you a chance to assess what you can do, and advice as to how to analyse your learning style. It will suggest ways you can build on what you already know. Bruner, cited in Thompson and Calder (1974), argued that all educators should have knowledge about learning, about teaching and about knowledge itself, and this view has since been confirmed, for instance in the Rumbold report (1990).

REFLECTION POINT 30 [1.6]

If you are aware of your strengths you can capitalise on them. You should also make the most of opportunities to work on skills that you don't feel you are achieving as effectively as you might.

How do you feel about your ability to process information? Assess yourself using the exercise below.

- Copy the study skills audit twice, and then complete one copy to gain an idea of how you view your strengths and weaknesses at the moment.
- Then put this copy aside.
- When you have finished reading this chapter you will need the second copy. Guidance will be given as to how to use this.

Study skills audit

For each section range your responses from 1 = very unsure through to 6 = very happy/confident.

I feel confident to:

Organise my time, and work to deadlines	1	2	3	4	5	6
Prioritise demands on my time	1	2	3	4	5	6
Read plans, policies and other school documents	1	2	3	4	5	6
Read articles from educational magazines/journals	1	2	3	4	5	6
Read textbooks	1	2	3	4	5	6
Read charts/graphs and statistical material	1	2	3	4	5	6
Use the library to locate specific books	1	2	3	4	5	6
Use the internet to research information	1	2	3	4	5	6
Take notes from books	1	2	3	4	5	6
Take notes while listening to someone speaking	1	2	3	4	5	6
Write a short factual report	1	2	3	4	5	6
Produce an piece of writing in which I discuss differing points of view	1	2	3	4	5	6
Voice my opinions in a small group	1	2	3	4	5	6
Talk to a large group	1	2	3	4	5	6

Learning styles

Watching children learn and develop is fascinating. It is very rewarding to feel that you have played a part in helping a child to reach a target. We are used to thinking about children learning but the current view of education is that 'learning is for all' and that we should all continue to learn throughout our lives. Estelle Morris, former Secretary for State for Education, emphasised the importance of creating opportunities for everyone to develop their learning, and encouraging and enabling adults to learn, improve their skills and enrich their lives (DfEE 2001).

I discovered, when revising for exams at about the age of 13, that I learn best by having to explain what I have learnt; in other words, re-presenting the facts and making them my own. It has been suggested that learning is not consolidated until we do this in some way. For both my GCEs (as they were then) and my A levels I taped notes, listened to them and then switched off and tried to speak those facts out loud. Do you know how you learn most effectively?

There are several ways of analysing learning styles. For instance we may consider that during any learning opportunity each person might experience a range of different stimuli, and will vary in their response to these. This way of thinking about learning styles is often referred to as VAK (visual, auditory, kinaesthetic), so for instance:

- some people seem to make pictures in their mind, and work well by consulting diagrams. They may learn better with visual cues. An example of the way pictures or gestures can help learners that you may have seen in school might be one of the systems used to support autistic children where simple drawings might be used to explain the daily routine, or to address desirable behaviour e.g. Makaton;
- some people need to hear explanations, sometimes phrased in several different ways. They may learn better with auditory cues;
- some need to incorporate movement into learning situations. They need kinaesthetic cues. A good example of kinaesthetics supporting learning is the Jolly Phonics scheme (Lloyd, 1992), which provides movements that the children learn in partnership with phonics to aid their memory.

In order to discover which is your preferred approach; visual, auditory or kinaesthetic, try the diagnostic exercise, which can be accessed and analysed via the internet. Information changes rapidly on the internet. You could try using a search engine such as **www.google.co.uk**, and inserting the words 'learning styles'. At the time of writing the following sites were rewarding:

www.open2.net/childofourtime/
www.metamath.com/lsweb/dvclearn.htm

Bernice McCarthy offers the following review of learning styles (**www.4Mat.com**):

Which of these fits you best?

The Innovative Learner:
- needs to be able to relate new content to personal experiences, and be able to see the relevance to real life;
- likes to be given reasons for learning and opportunities to combine areas of learning;
- enjoys being able to co-operate with fellow learners and to brainstorm ideas.

The Analytic Learner:

- needs to be able to hear about the content from those 'in the know';
- likes acquiring facts to widen their knowledge of ideas and processes;
- enjoys lectures and analysing data as well as researching independently.

The Common Sense Learner:

- needs to be able to see how things work;
- likes getting directly involved;
- enjoys hands-on tasks, experiential, concrete opportunities for learning.

The Dynamic Learner:

- needs to have opportunities to discover for themselves and to study independently;
- likes activities which involve simulations, role playing and games;
- enjoys teaching others as well as themselves.

These descriptions are related to David Kolb's (Abbot, 1994) research on learning.

REFLECTION POINT 31 [1.6] [2.5]

Try putting this awareness about yourself into practice by using the table below to make a list of three things you think you have learnt while working in school. Try to assess the strategies you used to do this.

I LEARNT:	I DID THIS BY:

Another way to reflect on what kind of learner you are, is to consider research by Howard Gardener (1984, at **www.acceleratedlearning.com/**). In his view you would not find yourself somewhere along the continuum between not intelligent and intelligent. Rather, you can be intelligent in different ways. He suggested seven perspectives, later extended to eight, which are referred to as Multiple Intelligences:

1. Linguistic
2. Logical/Mathematical/Scientific
3. Visual/Spatial
4. Musical
5. Bodily/Physical/Kinaesthetic
6. Naturalistic
7. Inter-personal
8. Intra-personal

You could make a profile for yourself that shows that you have developed each of the above, though at differing rates and levels or test yourself free at the website address above. The way you think and behave as a learner would depend on the inter-play between your intelligences, and the way learning opportunities were presented. Using methods which immerse the learner in experiences and which play to a variety of intelligences, is likely to lead to more successful learning. If you think your strengths lie in musical and linguistic areas, and you want to learn particular facts, arranging these into rhyming couplets with a strong rhythm might be an effective way to remember. Here is an example of a rhyme I made quite quickly to help remember how to spell three words which all sound the same and which are commonly misspelt.

> There, for pointing, e-r-e
> Over there, can't you see?
> Their, for owning, e-i-r
> That small red one is their car
> They're is the way to say 'they be'
> Cuts 'a' from 'are' leaving y'r-e

Study skills

The term 'study skills' can be used to describe a number of different processes (Nortledge, 1990: 16). The first of these he describes as habits of work, which this section will focus on first. Nortledge also suggests that the term 'study skills' encompasses techniques, strategies and understanding. In order to explain the distinction between these he uses the example of developing skills on the computer:

- **techniques** would include *how to save a document, how to underline words, and how to cut a section of text and 'paste' it elsewhere* (ibid: 17);

- **strategies** would include *how to use the storing and filing capabilities of the computer, how to get it to help you with the structuring of your documents*;
- **understanding** is where more of a general knowledge of how the processes in a computer work is developed. *To do this you would need to develop 'ideas' or 'models' in your mind of how a computer works. This requires reading manuals...and 'playing around' seeing what happens if....This type of learning is very different from learning how to touch type'* (ibid: 18).

What follows will help guide you through some of the habits, techniques and strategies you will be working on. The understanding will follow with practise, and is something unique to each person.

Organising for study

As a TA you are likely to be experienced at juggling priorities at home and at work. Carrying out reading and research, whether for a course or not, requires that you have to think of yourself, at least for some of the time.

Habits, techniques and strategies

Top tip 1: Having a place to work, so that you don't have to clear away, can make a big difference to progress

Whatever your situation you need to consider where you will work. If you are fortunate enough to have a study or study area then this will seem straightforward. If not, the kitchen or dining room table or the spare bedroom might be identified as a likely space. None of these are without complications though – having to clear away for dinner just when the words are flowing can be very frustrating. If you are using the computer your choice may be limited. Talking this over early on with those you live with may avert a crisis later on!

Top tip 2: Making a regular time that everyone knows will be your time for studying at home and/or at school will help you plan to meet deadlines

There are many challenges to organising even a normal day. At home, if you are going to fit in time for study, in which you have to concentrate for a sustained period, you may have to compromise over some things. It will be useful, however, for those who have a call on you to accept that at a particular time you need 'space'. If you are a parent, seeing you studying can be a powerful role model to the offspring! You may have research to carry out while at school. It is important to negotiate this with your line manager beforehand, so that everyone is clear about your needs.

Top tip 3: Organising as much support as possible for yourself will ensure you remain as stress-free as possible

You will appreciate support from whatever quarter.

- If you can organise those you live with to take on some of the regular jobs, to alleviate pressure from you, this will help. Consider any shortcuts that are open to you in your situation – for instance it may be appropriate to shop on-line.

- If you are enrolled on a course you may need to have a mentor in your work place. Even if this is not a necessity it is a good idea to explain what you are doing to a colleague. This could be the Head, the SENCO, the teacher you work with most, or another TA – perhaps one who has also studied recently. They may be in a position to help you negotiate aspects of your timetable, if necessary, or arrange for opportunities to carry out work-based research.

Talking over issues with someone 'in the know' can help you clarify matters in your own mind. Having someone proof-read your work is a very sensible course of action, even if this is only to check grammar and spelling. Opening up to someone that you know personally or professionally can be a risky business – you are bound to feel vulnerable. If you can get over this feeling the advantages of having others realise how hard you are working are worth it. Schools are, of course, busy places so try to fix a regular meeting, because establishing even half an hour a week that is yours makes all the difference. Even if you don't meet then, you will both be aware that there is time 'on account'. I always give this advice to mentors and students. It's not uncommon for people to feel that what they would like to share is not important enough to merit bothering their mentor!

Top tip 4: Thinking methodically, planning ahead and scheduling targets or goals that you can achieve realistically will keep you going and enable you to meet deadlines

We all work to targets, in both our personal and professional lives. Maybe you set deadlines for yourself already. Perhaps you write 'to do' lists, or keep a calendar or a diary. If you do have a system in place you may need to extend it or formalise it somewhat. Consider giving yourself a written schedule, but break targets into small steps – this strategy is probably familiar from your work at school with children. It works for everybody! Being able to tick or cross out something you have achieved is a boost to the ego, and gives you the motivation to go on. Sometimes tasks seem insurmountable when you look at the whole picture, and are only manageable by meeting goals along the way. This is as significant professionally, where you may have been given responsibility for a long-term task, as it is to studying. Planning time ahead, maybe even with the use of a timetable, could also help when more than one person would like to use the computer, for instance. Being methodical and/or logical will help. The use of an alphabetical filing box to keep track of references and materials you are using is a good idea, or set up a file on the computer for this if you can. One of the biggest revelations to me has been gaining an understanding of how folders work on the computer. Imagine you want to put a photograph away safely. You put it on a page in an album, which is in a boxed collection of albums, which are on a shelf, in a cupboard, in a room in your house. You can do the same with the computer as long as you label all the stages of storage logically.

Writing skills

You may be asked to write reports or observations as part of your job, or you may be studying for a course where you are required to submit assignments for assessment towards certification. Some of the advice below could be useful for any of these purposes. It is important to determine your audience and your objectives. Writing a letter or diary entry is very different from writing in an academic way. Most of the writing you do as part of your profession or course will require a formal style. This is similar to the way we all adapt our speech according to whom we're talking. The example below is written as if the observer is talking to a friend. It might work as part of a collection of diary entries for some courses, but would not be acceptable as part of an essay for a Higher Education course.

> *I was working with Ryan. He has problems seeing well, and uses lots of things to help him learn. Today he was using his portable word processor. He's pretty good at putting things right as he went along and he could keep up with all the others as he gets to practise quite often – the weekly slots he has with Steve have helped a lot and he whizzes around the keyboard now.*

REFLECTION POINT 33 [2.6] [3.2.4]

Try and rephrase the wording of the same incident to create a formal report. Then compare your version with the one in Appendix 3.

Professional or academic writing should be free of emotive or judgmental language.

In your writing you will want to support your views or provide a basis for discussion using your reading as evidence. This can be done by referring to work. For example:

Bruce and Megitt (2000, p.185) point out the importance of a sense of self-esteem ...

Or by inserting a quotation, for example:

finding ways to improve the way he feels about himself may help build confidence. This view is endorsed by Bruce and Meggitt (2000, p.84), who point out that 'The way children feel about themselves and their bodies is deeply linked with self-confidence. This develops in children as they feel unconditionally valued, respected and to be of worth'.

Following a consistent method of referencing is important; the Harvard system is one system most commonly in use.

- In the text you should include the author's name, year of publication and page number.
- In the bibliography sources should be listed alphabetically, by surname, followed by year of publication, edition, (if appropriate), title, publisher name and place of publishing.

Sandy Green (2000) gives detailed advice on variations if you want to find out about referencing in more depth. Care should be taken to ensure that direct quotations are succinct.

Beginning an assignment

There are three main stages to address before you begin writing. You need to:

- decide what you have been asked to do;
- make a plan;
- carry out your research and assemble the evidence that you will use.

Deciding what you have been asked to do

The wording of the assignment title, and any instructions that follow are very important. To be successful it is crucial that you answer the question in the manner you have been requested to do, rather than recording all you know on the subject. You will need to read the brief you have been given carefully, several times. It will help to talk about the title with other students, or with your mentor. To decide what you need to do:

- Identify process words. These are words that tell you how you should deal with the content of the assignment – for instance, 'discuss', 'compare', 'describe', 'illustrate'. Check that you understand what the words in your assignment title mean.
- Identify content words. These are words that indicate what is essential to include in your work e.g. 'national curriculum', 'policies'.
- Read the complete question and try to explain to yourself exactly what you think you must do by the end of your work.
- Note any theories or ideas that immediately appear to you to be relevant.

> **REFLECTION POINT 33** [2.6]
>
> Underline the words that you think will be most significant in dealing with this essay title.
>
> *How can ICT be used to support and enhance learning? Answer with reference to practical case study material from your own experience, and to current educational thinking.*
>
> Compare your analysis with the one suggested in Appendix 3.

Making a plan

Writing your assignment will be comparatively straightforward if you have a clear plan to work from. It's a little like decorating – the end product is all the more professional if the preparation is done thoroughly. To make a plan you will need to:

● brainstorm the content of the assignment – any method will do, but many people find spider diagrams or mind maps helpful. Include any examples or references that you are already aware of;

● sort this material into a logical order, deciding what will go in your introduction, what will go in the conclusion, and identifying a sensible number of sections for the main body of your writing. You may need to review this when you have completed your research;

● check that you have included all the information you had thought of;

● check that your organisation and chosen structure will enable the question to be answered effectively.

Carrying out research

Most assignments will require you to use a balance of examples from secondary sources (books, articles, and data from tests or OFSTED reports, for example) and from primary sources, such as your own observations of children, or the results of surveys/questionnaires that you have carried out. There are publications which can advise on methods of collecting data from primary research in more detail than is possible here, for instance Diane Montgomery's book, (2002) which has a good chapter on classroom observation.

Reading

If you are studying at Higher Education level you will need to read extensively. Some reading will be directed reading, provided alongside coursework, but you will also need to research independently. If there is a book list provided this can serve as a starting point, though don't think of it as definitive – there are many useful sources; articles in magazines, newspapers, and material found on the internet, for instance.

Top tip 5: Keep a record of the reading you have undertaken so that you can return to it or refer to it later

How do I locate useful reading material?

Books: One book can offer valuable clues to other books and source material. Consult the bibliography for a list of related titles and sources that may be worth following up.

Schools: These very often have a collection of books and other source material available for staff reference. This will often be very useful for practical ideas, and designing materials for use with children. Schools will also have publications from bodies such as OFSTED and QCA. They often invest in periodicals such as *Child Education* (published by Scholastic). Colleagues may be able to lend or recommend books, especially if they have studied recently.

Libraries: You will be able to borrow from the college library if you are registered on a course. Sometimes the library at your college may not be specialised enough, but it is worth finding out if they are members of UK Libraries Plus. This is a scheme which allows certain students who are registered with the library in one institution access to the resources of up to two other libraries attached to institutions which normally lend to their students exclusively. If your library is not a member of such a scheme, or you are not, at present, registered on a course which allows this, there may be other routes worth pursuing. For instance libraries will often allow people to pay to become 'external readers', and if you are a full-time employee of the local authority this may be a reasonable fee.

Libraries are normally organised using the Dewey system, which you might be familiar with from school, or elsewhere. This divides subjects by type and by number. Specialist libraries may use a different system e.g. Bliss, which uses numbers, plus a combination of letters from subject and author. Most libraries give induction sessions, which you should make the most of. It is worthwhile becoming familiar with the system and practising locating books by using the search screens that most provide. All books carry ISBN numbers, found on the back of the publication, which can be helpful in identifying books (at bookshops, too).

Top tip 6: The internet [2.4]

There is a wealth of information on the World Wide Web but searches can be very time-consuming. Government documents and research reports are often available for downloading from the internet. Try accessing official education sites such as OFSTED, QCA, and National Curriculum. Try sites affiliated to the main educational unions. Also try using a search engine, such as **www.google.co.uk** where you can search by using keywords.

Reading purposefully

When you begin to research a subject it is very easy to become engrossed in one particular area, or to 'go off at a tangent', and spend too much of your time reading material that won't contribute a great deal to your cause. Firstly, then, you should have a good idea of how much time you have available to research the task in hand. Then you can decide where you are going to look, and in how much depth, and so on.

To maximise effort while reading:

● Make use of the Contents page and the index to get an idea of whether a book is going to be useful and then which sections to look at.

- Set clear objectives regarding what you wish to find out, and keep re-reading these objectives at regular intervals to keep yourself on task.

- Read with a pencil in your hand. You will be actively engaged, and therefore take in more. If you are reading a book belonging to you, or a newspaper article, you could underline key parts. Otherwise make notes as you go (including references), possibly using a card index file or notebook with divisions. You could also use a computer database, though this may restrict where you read.

- Question yourself regularly e.g., Do I agree with this? Does my experience match with this?

- Skim read sections first, and then decide whether to read in more detail.

- Scan for particular information – for instance look for names of theorists or concepts.

The purpose of reading is not to remember everything you read, but to understand ideas, recall some of those ideas, and to construct your own views from these. The purpose of note taking is to help you sort out meaning. If it becomes laborious it will serve little purpose.

REFLECTION POINT 34 [2.6]

Read through all these instructions before beginning.

1. Turn to Appendix 3 and locate the paragraph of reading for this reflection point.

2. Cast your eyes over it quickly and close the page. Which are the two Educators mentioned in the extract? If you can answer this you were scanning efficiently.

3. Open the page again and take a few moments to consider the structure and purpose. Close the extract. Can you now say how many main points the author is making? Have you worked out what the purpose of the extract is?

4. Read the extract carefully. Now make a mind map which summarises the critique offered. Compare yours to the one which follows the extract in the Appendix.

Writing an assignment

Writing takes practice, especially when you haven't done it for a long time. With practice you will develop strategies for approaching assignments and a style of your own, and the process will become more fluid and manageable. You need to expect to write a first draft, and then edit this, maybe several times, though this will be easier if you are confident at word processing. Word limits can help to create balance in your work. As a rough guide to begin with allow yourself around 20–25% of the words for the introduction and conclusion, and divide the rest sensibly between sections in the main body of your work. With practice you will get a feel for varying this when necessary. To put your writing together effectively ask yourself whether you have:

- written a clear introduction which sets out your objectives;
- used separate paragraphs for each main idea or piece of information, and side headings where appropriate (not too many – just for the main ideas);
- acknowledged all your references and referenced your quotations correctly;
- included a bibliography;
- included an appendix if appropriate – only include relevant material to which you have directly referred;
- numbered your pages;
- used double spacing and an acceptable font size and style;
- expressed yourself clearly. Proof-read and amend any phrases that sound as if you are talking to a friend. Use transition words/phrases like 'however', 'similarly', and 'on the other hand it can be argued that' to link ideas and make your work flow;
- explained your points clearly. Imagine that you are writing for someone with an interest but without course knowledge, such as a governor from your school;
- checked that you have shown you are aware of equal opportunities and have not used any biased terms;
- drawn together the main points in your conclusion.

Making an essay meet requirements

Although the description of criteria may vary from institution to institution or even from each piece of work you do, the reader is likely to consider aspects of the following:

- Presentation
- Theory
- Application
- Reflection

Presentation

This will include the way you structure your work as well as the clarity with which you communicate the content.

Structure

- An introduction which addresses the question and sets out clear objectives and explains how you will deal with your work in the main body of the assignment.
- A balanced piece of writing which develops your ideas and shows that you understand theories, models and arguments that you have been introduced to, and can relate these to your practical experiences in a critical fashion. The use of side headings to define your sections is advisable for most assignments.

- A conclusion, which refers back to your introduction, to your objectives, and shows how you have fulfilled these. You should also make some recommendations and/or state your own opinions in the light of your discussion.

Clarity

- Writing which is grammatically correct and spell-checked. Proof-reading is crucial. Try to identify colloquialisms, for instance, and choose an alternative way of explaining your meaning.
- Writing which adopts an appropriate style – in a formal essay you need to imagine you are speaking to someone like your bank manager rather than your friend. A sense of audience is important. Try to assume that the reader of your work will not know about the course – you need to explain clearly as if they have no prior knowledge of what you have been researching.
- Work which is presented within the guidelines given – there may be conventions regarding margin widths, spacing and so on. Check what the policy is and keep to it.

Theory

Education is full of theories, ideas, models and arguments. Whatever you are writing about you will need to demonstrate that you can link what you have learned at college, and what you know from your practical work, with the theories and ideas of writers working in the area you have been studying.

You need to include:

- references and quotations which support or illustrate a point you are making;
- evidence of the ability to be critical in your evaluation of what you have read;
- a range of sources, not just one or two books;
- correctly listed references and sources within your bibliography.

Application

This is a crucial area, especially for courses which place emphasis on work-related activities and the knowledge gained from them. The links between ideas and practice go both ways. It is just as important to analyse and evaluate your own practical work as it is to analyse what you read. You should try to develop:

- the ability to choose and use examples from practice, analysing these in the light of theories;
- presentation of evidence of evaluation of your own practice and practice of others that you have observed;
- an awareness of how your learning is affecting your practice;

- the ability to critically evaluate situations and suggest a course of action for the future;
- an understanding that there is more than one way to achieve success.

Reflection

The ability to probe ideas, and to weigh up different views or theories is a key skill at Higher Education level. Good description is essential, but you need to go beyond this and demonstrate an ability to be critical, to think, and to reflect on what you have seen, done and read. Effective reflection includes:

- evidence that you have considered, and drawn upon course material, research you have conducted from books and articles, and practical material;
- examples of thinking and research which demonstrate your ability and interest, which may develop beyond the material you have been directed to consider within the course;
- an understanding that evaluation may often be about the significance of values – the ability to stand back from an issue and to identify where ideas have come from, and their significance to theoretical models;
- the ability to appreciate the wider context of specific issues;
- the ability to reflect on your own progress, on your views and your experiences.

Recording your learning: the reflective journal

Learning is a journey with both easy and difficult phases where you experience elation and deflation! Keeping a learning journal supports you along the way and provides a record of your progress, which helps you to reflect, review and refine your activities for more rewarding study. So how do you go about this process?

Starting your journal

Your journal is your own personal diary where you record your thoughts and experiences on what you are undergoing. An increasing number of students find this an essential prop for learning which provides them with a structure for thinking and sharing views in a focused way.

Buy yourself one of those gorgeous hard-backed books that you can now find in stationery shops and which will entice you to pick it up and use it constantly. A hard-backed book is important as you are less likely to lose pages from it as you might from a ring binder file. If it looks and feels attractive you will always want your journal with you to make you feel good!

Use your journal as often as you like to record your views on something you have read or experienced. At regular intervals (such as once a week) summarise what you feel you have learnt during this period and define what you think your next step will be in your study programme. Your brain develops and deepens its understanding of a topic or task by connecting up information and this simple process of taking regular stock of what you are achieving will improve and speed up your progress.

When I was at senior school we were required to write a brief reflection of what each lesson meant to us and share this with a neighbour. This simple technique encouraged us to become engaged with a lesson topic and sharpened our understanding as we had to tell others what we had absorbed. I am sure it was not a coincidence that students achieved excellent results from the school. We had educators who really understood the importance of bringing together learning in an active, systematic and sharing format so that our brains had a chance to lay down strong topic outlines on which to map on details when appropriate. If you want to explore the topic further, read *Lend us your ears: listen and learn* (Sage, 2003).

Remember Top tip 5, above. It is crucial to make sure you record the details of anything you have read – title, author, publisher and date of publication – either in the back of your journal, or in a card index system. This is very important as you can spend hours searching for the specifics of something you vaguely remember reading for that vital quote or piece of evidence needed for an assignment or dissertation. Successful learners are those who understand their own effective working methods and establish an easy, systematic method of recording facts and personal evaluations. This is a significant step, which will develop confidence in yourself as an effective learner and it is a necessary process in gaining the evaluative skill which will bring you high standard performances. So, plan that shopping trip now and buy the most beautiful book that you can find!

Moving forward

You have worked through a number of exercises to help develop improved skills in studying. Now is the time to make yourself a plan of action to address those aspects you would like to improve on.

Before you do, try to assess yourself again using the audit that appears at the beginning of this chapter, **without looking at your first assessment**.

Note those aspects you have scored more highly and value this achievement. Interestingly, there may be elements that you scored lower than the first time. Sometimes this is as a result of the realisation that there is so much more to know. Approach these, in particular, with a positive attitude and in the light of the work you have done, plan a few manageable targets. Give yourself a date to try to achieve these. When the date arrives review any movement and make a new plan.

I WANT TO IMPROVE IN:	I'M GOING TO TRY TO:	BY	REVIEW	FUTURE ACTION
Note taking	Focus on key words and use mind mapping	October (6 weeks time)	• Time it takes to read articles • Whether I can remember main points to tell someone else	

Summary

This section has introduced you to some of the issues that have to be considered if you want to achieve success in your studies. Try to clarify your own personal learning style and make sure that you have the best conditions for study. As a busy person with probably a job, home and family to consider, your time for study is limited and precious. Making a study plan and keeping to it is a priority. Put in some slippage so that if you are ill or other concerns take over for a spell your study plan can cope with this. Sometimes you have to adjust your life and perhaps set your alarm an hour earlier and fit in a study hour while your place is quiet and undisturbed. Everyone will have different priorities and opportunities in their lives and study has to fit your particular needs and circumstances.

Learning how to write an assignment will be an important worry and course materials will usually offer guidance. Having a clear question to answer and a knowledge of some literature to contextualise your topic is the way to start. Establish the evidence that will answer your question and finally stamp your own views on what you have presented. Developing a clear structure to your writing is the key to a successful piece of work and, like a new recipe, is not complicated once you have had your first try out and have understood what is required of you.

The most important thing is to enjoy your new opportunities to learn. They will take you to places you have only dreamt about if you develop your confidence and have faith in your ability. Good luck and good learning!

Take time to reflect on the main points that have been covered in this chapter.

- Successful study depends on knowing your learning preferences and providing for these.
- Developing a study plan with some slippage for things that might throw you off course occasionally is the key to a step by step approach that will ensure your success.
- Keeping a learning journal will support and encourage your learning journey and provide a record of your achievement.

- Get your head around assignment requirements and think of them as a new dish where you have to master the ingredients required (content) and follow the recipe (structure) in order to produce the perfect product.
- Enjoy your studies and make them happy and rewarding experiences so that they are a pleasure rather than a chore.

Appendix 1: HLTA standards

Professional values and practice for Higher Level Teaching Assistants (HLTA)

Standards cover both knowledge and understanding, and teaching and learning.

Those aiming for HLTA status must demonstrate competence in the standards in the following table. Activities in the book have been cross referenced to the standards and the numbers for each standard will be found adjacent to each activity, tip or reflection point throughout the text (e.g. [1.1]).

STANDARD NUMBER	DESCRIPTION	ACTIVITY	REFERENCE
1.1	Have high expectations of all pupils; respect their social, cultural, linguistic, religious and ethnic backgrounds; and are committed to raising their educational achievement.	Successful class interaction	Chapter 2
		Reflection point 15 Locating the number of different groups a child belongs to	Chapter 2
		Reflection point 16 Developing thinking through questioning	Chapter 3
		Reflection point 18 The most important things a school should educate its pupils in	Chapter 4
1.2	Build and maintain successful relationships with pupils, treat them consistently, with respect and consideration, and are concerned for their development as learners.	Reflection point 15 Locating the number of different groups a child belongs to	Chapter 2
		Top tip 1 The TA role: listening, controlling, questioning and explaining	Chapter 3
		Yourself as a communicator	Chapter 3 & Appendix 3

▶

STANDARD NUMBER	DESCRIPTION	ACTIVITY	REFERENCE
		Finding out about children's difficulties with school	Chapter 3
		Top tip 2 Deal effectively with difficult behaviour	Chapter 3
		Top tip 6 Produce explanations that are understood	Chapter 3
1.3	Demonstrate and promote the positive values, attitudes and behaviour they expect from the pupils with whom they work.	Reflection point 4 Professional practice and working with all pupils	Chapter 1
		Turning negative comments into positive ones	Chapter 3
		Top tips 3, 4, 5 Reframe requests positively, mirror behaviour, question effectively	Chapter 3
		Reflection point 25 The hidden curriculum	Chapter 4
1.4	Work collaboratively with colleagues, and carry out their roles effectively, knowing when to seek help and advice.	Reflection point 1 Changes to the role of the TA	Chapter 1
		Reflection point 2 Job titles and perceptions	Chapter 1
		Reflection point 5 The TA role: relationships with colleagues	Chapter 1
		Reflection point 8 The school team	Chapter 1

STANDARD NUMBER	DESCRIPTION	ACTIVITY	REFERENCE
		Yourself as a communicator	Chapter 3 & Appendix 3
		Reflection point 17 Exploring your own attitudes	Chapter 3
1.5	Liaise sensitively and effectively with parents and carers, recognising their roles in pupils' learning.	Top tip 1 TA role: listening, controlling, questioning and explaining	Chapter 3
		Yourself as a communicator	Chapter 3 & Appendix 3
		Analysis of body posture	Chapter 3
		Reflection point 17 Exploring your own attitudes	Chapter 3
		Check before you speak and act	Chapter 3
1.6	Improve their own practice, including through observation, evaluation and discussion with colleagues.	The role of the TA *is* serious work	Chapter 1
		Reflection point 3 Considering training opportunities	Chapter 1
		Reflection point 9 The TA role: job descriptions	Chapter 1
		Mina's role	Chapter 3
		Reflection point 17 Exploring your own attitudes	Chapter 3
		Reflection point 18 The most important things a school should educate its pupils in	Chapter 4

STANDARD NUMBER	DESCRIPTION	ACTIVITY	REFERENCE
		Reflection point 28 Clarifying terminology	Chapter 4
		Reflection point 29 Using the internet to consider policy and practice	Chapter 4
		Reflection point 30 Assess your ability to process information	Chapter 5
		Reflection point 31 Assessing your learning strategies	Chapter 5
2.1	Have sufficient understanding of their specialist area to support pupils' learning, and are able to acquire further knowledge to contribute effectively and with confidence to the classes in which they are involved.	Reflection point 3 Considering training opportunities	Chapter 1
		Reflection point 21 Observing a literacy/numeracy lesson and monitoring children's involvement	Chapter 4
		Reflection point 22 Considering opportunities for augmenting the Literacy or Numeracy Strategy	Chapter 4
		Reflection point 28 Clarifying terminology	Chapter 4
2.2	Are familiar with the school curriculum, the age-related expectations of pupils, the main teaching methods and the testing/examination frameworks in the subjects and age ranges in which they are involved.	Reflection point 7 The whole curriculum	Chapter 1
		Reflection point 10 Motor development	Chapter 2
		Reflection point 11 Brain development	Chapter 2
		Reflection point 13 Assessing development against a model	Chapter 2

STANDARD NUMBER	DESCRIPTION	ACTIVITY	REFERENCE
		Reflection point 14 Assessing language development against a model	Chapter 2
		Reflection point 18 The most important things a school should educate its pupils in	Chapter 4
		Reflection point 19 Analyse your school prospectus	Chapter 4
		Reflection point 21 Observing a literacy/ numeracy lesson and monitoring children's involvement	Chapter 4
		Reflection point 27 Analysing the purpose of assessment	Chapter 4
2.3	Understand the aims, content, teaching strategies and intended outcomes for the lessons in which they are involved, and understand the place of these in the related teaching programme.	Reflection point 6 The advantages and disadvantages of topic work	Chapter 1
		Reflection point 18 The most important things a school should educate its pupils in	Chapter 4
		Reflection point 19 Analyse your school prospectus	Chapter 4
		Reflection point 23 The observed curriculum v. the intended curriculum	Chapter 4
2.4	Know how to use ICT to advance pupils' learning, and can use common ICT tools for their own and pupils' benefit.	Reflection point 29 Using internet to consider policy and practice	Chapter 4
		Top tip 6 Using the internet for research	Chapter 5

▶

STANDARD NUMBER	DESCRIPTION	ACTIVITY	REFERENCE
2.5	Know the key factors that can affect the way pupils learn.	Reflection point 10 Motor development	Chapter 2
		Reflection point 11 Brain development	Chapter 2
		Patterns of responses: adult to child	Chapter 2
		Reflection point 15 Locating the number of different groups a child belongs to	Chapter 2
		Reflection point 31 Assessing your learning strategies	Chapter 5
2.6	Have achieved a qualification in English/literacy and mathematics/numeracy, equivalent to at least Level 2 of the National Qualifications Framework	Reflection point 32 Writing a formal report	Chapter 5
		Reflection point 33 Analysing an essay title	Chapter 5
		Reflection point 34 Skim reading and scanning	Chapter 5
2.7	Are aware of the statutory frameworks relevant to their role.	Reflection point 20 National Curriculum subjects and their distribution/time allocation	Chapter 4
2.8	Know the legal definition of Special Educational Needs (SEN), and are familiar with the guidance about meeting SEN given in the SEN Code of Practice.	Integration for Matthew	Chapter 1
		Inclusion: a potted history	Chapter 1/ Appendix 1
2.9	Know a range of strategies to establish a purposeful learning environment and to promote good behaviour.	Reflection point 12 Promoting appropriate attention levels	Chapter 2
		Top tip 2 Deal effectively with difficult behaviour	Chapter 3

STANDARD NUMBER	DESCRIPTION	ACTIVITY	REFERENCE
		Turning negative comments into positive ones	Chapter 3
		Top tips 3, 4, 5 Reframe requests positively, mirror behaviour, question effectively	Chapter 3
		Tips for top talkers	Chapter 3
3.1.1	Contribute effectively to teachers' planning and preparation of lessons.	Reflection point 20 National Curriculum subjects and their distribution/time allocation	Chapter 4
		Reflection point 26 Planning lessons and activities	Chapter 4
3.1.2	Working within a framework set by the teacher, plan their role in lessons including how they will provide feedback to pupils and colleagues on pupils' learning and behaviour.	Reflection point 8 The school team	Chapter 1
		Reflection point 22 Considering opportunities for augmenting the Literacy or Numeracy Strategy	Chapter 4
3.1.3	Contribute effectively to the selection and preparation of teaching resources that meet the diversity of pupils' needs and interests.	Reflection point 4 Professional practice and working with all pupils	Chapter 1
		Setting up activities where a pupil has to explain to others	Chapter 3
		Check before you speak and act	Chapter 3
3.1.4	Contribute to the planning of opportunities for pupils to learn in out-of-school contexts, in accordance with school policies and procedures.	Reflection point 19 Analyse your school prospectus	Chapter 4

▶

STANDARD NUMBER	DESCRIPTION	ACTIVITY	REFERENCE
		Reflection point 24 The whole curriculum: provision for children with artistic, musical or sporting abilities	Chapter 4
3.2.1	Are able to support teachers in evaluating pupils' progress through a range of assessment activities.	Reflection point 13 Assessing development against a model	Chapter 2
		Reflection point 14 Assessing language development against a model	Chapter 2
		Reflection point 23 The observed curriculum v. the intended curriculum	Chapter 4
		Reflection point 27 Analysing the purpose of assessment	Chapter 4
3.2.2	Monitor pupils' responses to learning tasks and modify their approach accordingly.	Reflection point 13 Assessing development against a model	Chapter 2
		Patterns of responses: adult to child	Chapter 2
		Reflection point 14 Assessing language development against a model	Chapter 2
		Reflection point 16 Developing thinking through questioning	Chapter 3
		Top tip 6 Produce explanations that are understood	Chapter 3
		Top tip 7 Use gestures to aid expression	Chapter 3
		Analysis of body posture	Chapter 3

STANDARD NUMBER	DESCRIPTION	ACTIVITY	REFERENCE
3.2.3	Monitor pupils' participation and progress, providing feedback to teachers, and giving constructive support to pupils as they learn.	Reflection point 12 Promoting appropriate attention levels	Chapter 2
		Finding out about children's difficulties with school	Chapter 3
		Top tip 6 Produce explanations that are understood	Chapter 3
		Reflection point 21 Observing a literacy/ numeracy lesson and monitoring children's involvement	Chapter 4
3.2.4	Contribute to maintaining and analysing records of pupils' progress.	Reflection point 27 Analysing the purpose of assessment	Chapter 4
		Reflection point 32 Writing a formal report	Chapter 5
3.3.1	Using clearly structured teaching and learning activities, interest and motivate pupils, and advance their learning.	Reflection point 16 Developing thinking through questioning	Chapter 3
3.3.2	Communicate effectively and sensitively with pupils to support their learning.	Successful class interaction	Chapter 2
		Top tip 1 TA role: listening, controlling, questioning and explaining	Chapter 3
		Yourself as a communicator	Chapter 3 & Appendix 3
		Turning negative comments into positive ones	Chapter 3
		Top tips 3, 4, 5 Reframe requests positively, mirror behaviour, question effectively	Chapter 3

▶

STANDARD NUMBER	DESCRIPTION	ACTIVITY	REFERENCE
3.3.3	Promote and support the inclusion of all pupils in the learning activities in which they are involved.	Reflection point 4 Professional practice and working with all pupils	Chapter 1
		Reflection point 15 Locating the number of different groups a child belongs to	Chapter 2
		Reflection point 25 The hidden curriculum	Chapter 4
3.3.4	Use behaviour management strategies, in line with the school's policy and procedures, which contribute to a purposeful learning environment.	Reflection point 4 Professional practice and working with all pupils	Chapter 1
		Top tip 2 Deal effectively with difficult behaviour	Chapter 3
		Top tip 3, 4,5 Reframe requests positively, mirror behaviour, question effectively	Chapter 3
3.3.5	Advance pupils' learning in a range of classroom settings, including working with individuals, small groups and whole classes where the assigned teacher is not present.	Reflection point 26 Planning lessons and activities	Chapter 4
3.3.6	Are able, where relevant, to guide the work of other adults supporting teaching and learning in the classroom.	Top tips 1 TA role: listening, controlling, questioning and explaining	Chapter 3
3.3.7	Recognise and respond effectively to equal opportunities issues as they arise, including by challenging stereotyped views, and by challenging bullying or harassment, following relevant policies and procedures.	Integration for Matthew	Chapter 1
		Reflection point 15 Locating the number of different groups a child belongs to	Chapter 2

STANDARD NUMBER	DESCRIPTION	ACTIVITY	REFERENCE
3.3.8	Organise and manage safely the learning activities, the physical teaching space and resources for which they are given responsibility.	Reflection point 8 Working with the school team	Chapter 1
		Top tip 2 Deal effectively with difficult behaviour	Chapter 3
		Reflection point 26 Planning lessons and activities	Chapter 4

1944 Education Act	Identified a number of categories of 'disability', but at the same time it was a commonly held belief that some children were uneducable in 'normal' schools and separate provision should be made for them. This was underpinned by the development of intelligence tests that gave a standard measure of IQ (Intelligence Quotient) and could therefore be used to determine a predicted level of achievement. In the early 1970s a move away from selection by ability gave rise to the comprehensive system within the secondary sector. As a result the realisation that it was also undesirable to select by disability or inability began to take hold.
1978 Warnock Report	Paved the way for inclusion by making significant changes to the way that children were assessed and helped. Introduced the concept of individual needs.
1981 Education Act	Recommended that, where possible, children with special educational needs should be included within mainstream provision, which was completely opposite to the stance that had been in place since 1944. For the first time there was a system of statementing children to provide for particular identified needs.
1988 National Curriculum	Enabled Special Needs children to be disapplied if appropriate.
1989 Children's Act	Every child given the right to protection from abuse and exploitation.
1993 Dearing Review	Built on the idea of appropriateness, making it acceptable for children to work at the correct level for them, and introduced the idea of small steps between levels so that progress could be shown for children whose rate of achievement was slower than average.
1994 Code of Practice	Clarified the five stages of statementing and made schools accountable for stages one to three and the LEAs accountable for levels four and five.
1995 Disability Act	Aimed to end discrimination against disabled people. It took effect in three stages, the last of which is scheduled for implementation in October 2004. Gave definition of disability. (**www.disability.gov.uk/dda/**) The DDA describes a disabled person as anyone *with a physical or mental impairment which has a substantial and long-term adverse effect upon his or her ability to carry out normal day-to-day activities*. Education exempted.

1996 Education Act	Part four deals with SEN. It details a Code of Practice with practical guidance on how to identify, assess, record, meet, and review SEN. Sets a limit of 26 weeks to complete the legal process and issue a statement that would be legally binding. Parents are able to express preferences. Schools are obligated to accept children and to have policies in place. (**www.hmso.gov.uk**)
1997 Green Paper 'Excellence for All Children: Meeting Special Needs'	Set goals to be met by 2002. Target setting began, explicitly taking into account the scope for achievement of children with SEN. It encouraged the use of ICT to support and enhance learning. It provided more training in SEN and EBD for all school personnel and a proposal of a National Framework for training of LSAs. It clarified IEPs, which must include pastoral and medical needs from now on. (**www.dfes.gov.uk/sengp**)
2001 Special Educational Needs and Disability Act Code of Practice (revised)	Children with Special Needs but no statement must be educated in mainstream schools. Those with statements should also be educated in mainstream schools unless this is against the parents' wishes or likely to affect the education of others. (**www.hmso.gov.uk**) It reduced SEN paperwork as a response to the overload of administrative duties for teachers, by, for instance, introducing group targets. It came into force from September 2002, when schools had to change discriminatory policies and practices. From 2003 there is an expectation that auxiliary aids and services will be provided where needed, and from 2005 (in education) 'reasonable' physical adjustments must be made.
2003 Green Paper 'Every Child Matters'	Sets out for consultation a framework for improving outcomes for all children and their families, to protect them, to promote their well-being, and to support all children to develop their full potential. Concentrates on four areas: <ul><li>supporting parents and carers;</li><li>early intervention and effective protection;</li><li>accountability and integration: locally, regionally and nationally;</li><li>workforce reform.</li></ul> (**www.dfes.gov.uk/everychildmatters/**)
2004 Removing Barriers to Achievement: The Government's Strategy for SEN	Building on the 2001 Act and 2003 Green Paper this reaffirms the commitment to a partnership of services caring for children with SEN and disability, giving opportunities to succeed in order that every child should fulfil their potential. It recognised that there is too much variation in present provision and that 1 in 6 children have some need. Education should be personalised and responsive. This includes early intervention and raising expectations. It initiates a new Inclusion Development Programme, linking with the national behaviour strategy. (**www.standards.dfes.gov.uk/literacy/publications/inclusion/883963/dfes011704_removebarrier.pdf**)

2004 Five Year Strategy for Children and Learners	*Every child making the best possible progress in reading, writing and maths, with high-quality teachers and support staff in the classroom giving children more tailored learning.* A repudiation of a *return to a system based on selection of the few and rejection of the many.* 'Foundation partnerships' are developed to enable schools to group together to raise standards and to work together to take on wider responsibilities in areas such as provision for special educational needs or hard-to-place pupils. **(www.dfes.gov.uk/publications/5yearstrategy)**

Appendix 3: Communication skills: answers to exercises

Chapter 3: Communication activities in Mina's story:

Conversation with parents and children before school

Taking the register

Previewing the day's activities

Calming the group with a story

Teaching a strategy to understand

Helping with a maths problem – scaffolding thinking and problem solving

Selling books in the bookshop

Vocabulary building in a literacy hour plenary session

Moderating behaviour in music time

Counselling and supporting an upset pupil

Making a presentation to a staff meeting

Negotiating with pupils with regard to a display of their transport models

Coaching Marcus

Explaining the game of rounders

Discussing with the class teacher the children's lack of attention

Taking story time

Reviewing the day and saying goodbyes to the children

Taking a COGS group

Explaining COGS to a PGCE student

Negotiating with the head with regard to a classroom observation

Tackling an assignment – reading and writing activities

Chapter 3: Thinking about your role: answers

LISTENING	CONTROLLING	QUESTIONING	EXPLAINING
HEARING	CRITICISING	REQUESTING	INFORMING
ATTENDING	DISAGREEING	SUGGESTING	CLARIFYING
LINKING	REQUIRING	PROPOSING	HELPING
RECALLING	DIRECTING	CONFIRMING	ASSISTING
UNDERSTANDING	INSTRUCTING	INVOLVING	CO-OPERATING
EMPATHISING	COUNSELLING	MOTIVATING	CONTRIBUTING

Chapter 3: How do you feel about your communication?

Name:.. Date:.............................

The following statements are concerned with aspects of life and communication. If a statement is mostly (75%) **true** for you circle the letter T. If the statement is **false** or not usually true for you, circle the letter F. Please try to answer all the statements.

1.	I am generally satisfied with my life	T	F
2.	I feel I have many good qualities	T	F
3.	I am often lonely	T	F
4.	I am generally upset by criticism	T	F
5.	I set my hopes low to avoid disappointment	T	F
6.	I delay things rather than deal with them immediately	T	F
7.	I am generally patient with other people	T	F
8.	If someone is rude to me I let it pass by	T	F
9.	I find it difficult to say NO to demands made on me	T	F
10.	I take charge of things if I have a chance	T	F
11.	I do not like change and variety in my life	T	F
12.	I am always well organised and on time for events	T	F
13	I find it difficult to finish off things I have started	T	F
14.	I worry about making a good impression on other people	T	F
15.	I find it difficult to relax	T	F
16.	I make decisions regardless of other people's opinion	T	F
17.	I like an ordered pattern to life	T	F
18.	I keep an open mind about things	T	F
19.	I like activities that involve mixing with other people	T	F
20.	I do not find it easy to show people I like them	T	F
21.	I make a favourable impression when I talk	T	F
22.	I do not find it easy to look at my audience while speaking to a group	T	F
23.	I enjoy giving a talk in public	T	F
24.	Some words are harder than others for me to say	T	F

25.	People sometimes seem uncomfortable when I am talking to them	T	F
26.	I dislike introducing one person to another	T	F
27.	I often ask questions in group discussions	T	F
28.	I find it easy to control my voice when speaking	T	F
29.	I do not talk well enough to do the kind of work I would really like to do	T	F
30.	I am not embarrassed by the way I talk	T	F
31.	I talk easily with only a few people	T	F
32.	I talk better than I write	T	F
33.	I often feel nervous when talking	T	F
34.	I find it hard to talk when I meet new people	T	F
35.	I feel confident about my speaking ability	T	F
36.	I wish I could say things as clearly as other people do	T	F
37.	Even though I know the right answer I often fail to give it because I am afraid to speak out	T	F
38.	I hesitate when asking information from other people	T	F
39.	I find it easy to talk to people on the telephone	T	F
40.	I forget about myself soon after I begin to speak	T	F

Look at the balance of positive and negative responses you have made. How can you turn a negative attitude into a positive one? For e.g: If you have marked statement 1 (I am generally satisfied with my life) as *false* (a negative response), think *why* you are not satisfied with your life. How will you seek to change this? Such a framework allows you to approach your self development in a systematic way.

Chapter 3: Answer to Miller's puzzle

Chapter 5: Reflection point 33

In today's literacy lesson I supported a child with visual impairment. Ryan is provided with several resources that have facilitated his access to the curriculum. One important piece of equipment he used was a portable word processor. This enabled him to complete his writing, self-correcting as he went along. It gave him a chance to work at the same pace and speed as the rest of the class. His typing speed was good, as he has practised regularly. He has a keyboard instructor working with him, teaching him new skills during weekly lessons, and he has become far more confident.

Chapter 5: Reflection point 34

How can ICT be used to support and enhance learning? Answer with reference to practical case study material from your own experience, and to current educational thinking.

Process words:

How. You are going to be explaining. In this instance the title implies that ICT always supports and enhances. This is a positive stance. You may feel that not all your experience is positive. You can and should present reservations, by addressing how ICT would be supportive/enhancing if used in other ways.

Answer with reference to. The title gives specific guidance as to two areas of source material for illustration, so you need to ensure you address both for full credit.

Support. Implies learning will happen, but that ICT can help where there may be problems, for example.

Enhance. Implies that access to ICT will do more for learning than otherwise, so accelerating learning might be an example to examine.

Content words:

ICT. What does this include in your experience? Define your understanding/interpretation of this term.

Learning. Implies gainful pursuit, possibly not 'playing', though playing could be a strategy for learning. You might need to explain what you take this to mean.

Practical case study material. Implies you have been working with a specified child/group of children and have collected evidence of their work, which you will need to refer to directly, and which will be presented in an appendix.

Current educational thinking. You will need to decide what this might include or ask for clarification, but it is likely that for full credit you probably need to be using knowledge of theories of learning or National Curriculum content, or making reference to current debates on the use of ICT, for instance.

Chapter 5: Extract for reflection point 33

Evaluation of Vygotsky's approach

There are several significant strengths of Vygotsky's theoretical approach. As he argued, children's cognitive development does depend importantly on the social context and on guidance provided by adults and other children. Piaget underestimated the importance of the social environment, and Vygotsky deserves credit for acknowledging the key role it plays in cognitive development. It follows from Vygotsky's approach that there should be major differences in cognitive development from culture to culture, whereas Piaget argued that children everywhere go through the same sequence of cognitive stages in the same order. There is some evidence for the universal stages emphasised by Piaget but there are also important cultural differences in cognitive development.

There are several limitations to Vygotsky's theoretical approach.

First, he has been criticised for exaggerating the importance of the social environment. Children's rate of cognitive development is determined by their level of motivation and interest in learning, as well as by the social support they receive. Second, the account he offered is rather sketchy. He did not make it clear precisely what kinds of social interaction were most beneficial for learning (e.g., general encouragement versus specific instructions). According to Durkin (1995), the followers of Vygotsky 'offer only superficial accounts of how language is actually used in the course of social interactions'.

Third, social interactions between, for example, parent and child do not always have beneficial effects. Indeed, social interactions can make matters worse rather than better. As Durkin (1995) pointed out, 'People confronted with an opposing point of view...dig their heels in, get hot under the collar, refuse to budge, exploit their knowledge as a source of power and control, and so on.'

Fourth, Vygotsky assumed that social interactions enhanced cognitive development because of the instruction that was provided. However, there are other reasons why children benefit from social interactions. Light et al. (1994) found on a computer-based task that children learned better in pairs than on their own, even when the other child was merely present and did not say anything. This is known as social facilitation, and occurs because the presence of others can have a motivational effect.

Fifth, it would seem from Vygotsky's account that nearly all learning should be fairly easy if children receive the appropriate help from adults and other children. In fact, young children often take months or years to master complex skills even when they are well supported in their schools and homes. This suggests that there are genuine constraints on children's learning that were ignored by Vygotsky.

Vygotsky developed his theory during the last 10 years of his life, before he died of tuberculosis at the tragically early age of 38. At least some of the weaknesses of his approach might have been resolved had he lived longer.

References

Chapter 1

DfEE (2001) *National Occupational Standards for Early Years Care and Education.* London: HMSO.

DfES (2001) *Education and Skills: Delivering Results. A Strategy to 2006.* Suffolk: DfES.

DfES (2000) *Working with Teaching Assistants: a good practice guide.* London: HMSO. www.gov.uk/teachingreforms/support

DfES (1997) *Excellence for All: Meeting Special Educational Needs: A Programme of Action.* London: HMSO Green Paper.

DfES/TTA (2002) *Qualifying to Teach: Professional Standards for Qualified Teacher Status.* London: DfES/TTA.

Farrell, P, Balshaw, M, and Polat, F (1999) *The Management, Role and Training of Learning Support Assistants.* London: DfEE.

Fox, G (1998) *A Handbook for Learning Support Assistants.* London: Fulton.

Gold, K (2001) *New Wave of Support. Times Educational Supplement.* 6 April.

Greene, K, Lee, B, Springhall, E and Bemrose, R (2002) *Administrative Support Staff in Schools: Ways Forward* (DfES Research Report 331). London: DfES.

Hancock, R and Swann, W *Classroom Assistants in Primary Schools, Employment and Deployment.* ESRC project: R000237803.

Lalkhen, Y and Norwich, B (1990) in McNamara and Moreton (1993) London: Fulton.

Lee, B and Mawson, C (1998) *A Survey of Classroom Assistants.* London: NFER.

Local Government National Training Organisation (2001) *National Occupational Standards for Teaching Assistants.* London: LGNTO.

Lorenz, S (2002) *First Steps in Inclusion.* London: Fulton.

McNamara, S and Moreton, G (1993) *Teaching Special Needs: Strategies and Activities for Children in the Primary School.* London: Fulton.

Merry, R (1998) *Successful Children, Successful Teaching.* Buckingham: Open University Press.

Morris, Estelle, 'The School of the Future will radically transform Learning'. Speech at BETT show, Olympia. 9 January 2002. News Centre at www.dfes.gov.uk

Moyles, J (1992) *Organising for Learning in the Primary Classroom.* Buckingham: Open University Press.

Moyles, J and Suschitzchy, W (1997) *Jills of all Trades: Classroom Assistants in KS1 Classes.* London: ATL.

OFSTED (1999) *A Review of Primary Schools in England 1994–8.* London: HMSO.

OFSTED (2002) *Teaching Assistants in Primary Schools: An Evaluation of the Quality and Impact of their Work Place.* HMI. www.ofsted.gov.uk/publications/index.cfm?fuseaction=pubs.summary&id=7

O'Grady, C (2001) Help, I Need Somebody. *Times Educational Supplement,* 30 March.

OU/Pricewaterhousecoopers (2001) *Teacher Workload Study: Final Report* [online]. Available: www.teachernet.gov.uk/workloadstudy [1 February, 2002]. Professional Association of Teachers (2000).

PAT/PANN Press release: 18/03/99. *A Career Ladder for Classroom Assistants.* www.pat.org.uk

Rose, J, Alexander, R and Woodhead, C (1992) *Curriculum Organisation and Classroom Practice in Primary Schools: A Discussion Paper.* London: DES.

Rosenthal, R and Jacobson, L (1968) *Pygmalion in the classroom: Teacher expectation and pupils' intellectual development.* New York: Rhineart and Winston.

Schwartz, C (ed.) (1993) *The Chambers Dictionary.* Edinburgh: Chambers Harrap.

Slater, J and Dean, C (2001) Proper jobs that need proper staff, *Times Educational Supplement.* 16 November.

Slater, J (2002) Time to Upgrade the Supporters? *Times Educational Supplement*, 22 March.

Teacher net. www.teachernet.gov.uk/wholeschool/

TTA 171/A355 (1999) *Career Ladder for Classroom Assistants.* Southampton: University of Southampton and Hampshire County Council.

TTA,QTS standards. www.tta.gov.uk/php/read.php?sectionid=103&articleid=519

Unison 2001, Newsletter to members. www.unison.org.uk, August 2002.

US Dept of Labor (2002) *Occupational Outlook Handbook* 2002–3 online at www.bls.gov/oco/ocos153.htm

Chapter 2

Ainsworth, MDS (1973) 'The development of infant–mother attachment', in BM Caldwell and HN Ricciuti (eds), *Review of Child Development Research* Vol.3, Chicago: University of Chicago Press.

Bandura, A (1973) *Aggression, a Social Learning Analysis.* Englewood Cliffs, NJ: Prentice Hall.

Bee, H (2000) *The Developing Child* (9th edn). London: Allyn and Bacon.

Bell, N (1991) *Visualizing and Verbalizing.* Paso Robles, CA: Academy of Reading Publications.

Bell, SM (1970) 'The development of the concept of object as related to infant-mother attachment'. *Child Development*, 41: 291–311.

Bennett, J, Gash, H, and O'Reilly, M (1998) 'Ireland: Integration as appropriate, segregation where necessary', in T Booth and M Ainscow (eds) *From Them to Us.* London: Routledge.

Binet, A and Simon, T (1916) *The Development of Intelligence in Children.* Baltimore: Williams & Wilkins.

Borke, H (1975) 'Piaget's mountains revisited: changes in the egocentric landscape', *Developmental Psychology*, 11: 240–3.

Bowlby, J (1969) Attachment and loss (Vol.1) *Attachment.* New York: Basic Books.

Brazelton, TB, Robey, JS and Collier, GA (1969) 'Infant development in the Zinacanteco Indians of southern Mexico', *Pediatrics*, 44: 274–93.

Bruner, JS, Olver, RR and Greenfield, PM (1966) (eds) *Studies in Cognitive Growth.* New York: Wiley.

Chomsky, N (1965) *Aspects of the theory of syntax.* Cambridge, Mass: MIT Press.

Cooper J, Moodley M and Reynell J (1978) *Helping Language Development.* London: EA Arnold.

Cortes JB and Gatti FM (1965) 'Physique and self description of temperament', *Journal of Consulting Psychology*, 20: 432–9.

Dale, PS (1976) *Language Development: Structure and Function* (2nd ed) New York: Holt, Rinehart & Winston.

Department for Education and Employment (DfEE) (1996) *Education Act.* Section 312: Special Educational Needs (SEN) section.

Department for Education and Skills (DfES) (2001) *Special Educational Needs Code of Practice.* London: DfES.

Diorio, D, Viau,V and Meaney, MJ (1993) 'The role of the medial prefrontal cortex in the regulation of hypothalmic-pituitary-adrenal responses to stress', *Journal of Neuroscience*, 13(9): 3839–47.

Erikson, EH (1963) *Childhood and Society.* New York: Norton.

Freire, P (1972) *Pedagogy of the Oppressed.* London: Penguin.

Freud, S (1960) *A General Introduction to Psychoanalysis.* New York: Washington Square Press.

Gardner, H (1983) *Frames of Mind: The Theory of Multiple Intelligences.* New York: Basic Books.

Gelernter, D (1994) *The Muse in the Machine, Computerizing the Poetry of Human Thought.* New York: Free Press.

Gesell, A and Thompson, H (1929) 'Learning and growth in identical twins: an experimental study by the method of co-twin control', *Genetic Psychology Monographs*, 6: 1–123.

Gibson, EJ (1969) *Principles of Perceptual Learning and Development.* New York: Appleton.

Goleman, D (1996) *Emotional Intelligence.* London: Bloomsbury.

Goodenough FL (1931) *Anger in Young Children.* Minneapolis: University of Minnesota Press.

Hunter-Carsch, M (1999) *Report on the Leicester Summer Literacy Scheme.* Leicester: University of Leicester.

Kagan, J (1965) 'Reflection-impulsivity and reading ability in primary grade children', *Child Development*, 609–28.

Kagan, J (1971) *Change and Continuity in Infancy.* New York: Wiley.

Kohlberg, L (1966) 'A cognitive-developmental analysis of children's sex-role concepts and attitudes', in EE Maccoby (ed.) *The Development of Sex Differences.* Stanford, CA: Stanford University Press.

Levinson, HN (1988) 'The cerebellar-vestibular basis of learning disabilities in children, adolescents and adults; hypothesis and study', *Perceptual Motor Skills*, 67: 983–1006.

Meadows, S (1993) *The Child as Thinker: the Development and Acquisition of Cognition in Childhood.* London: Routledge.

Merry, R (1998) *Successful Children, Successful Teaching.* Buckingham: Open University Press.

Merzenich, M (1995) 'Brain plasticity origins of human abilities and disabilities', Sixth symposium, Decade of the Brain Series, NIMH and the Library of Congress, Washington DC, (7 February).

Piaget, J (1964) 'Development and learning', in R Ripple and V Rockcastle (eds) *Piaget Rediscovered.* Ithaca, NY: Cornell University Press, pp. 7–19.

Piaget, J and Inhelder, B (1969) *The Psychology of the Child.* New York: Basic Books.

Robson, A (1989) *Special Needs and Special Educational Needs*. London: paper published by the Inner London Education Authority.

Sage, R (2000) *Class Talk*. Stafford: Network Educational Press.

Sage, R (2003) *Lend Us Your Ears*. Stafford: Network Educational Press.

Sage, R (2004) *A World of Difference: Tackling Inclusion in Schools*. Stafford: Network Educational Press.

Sheldon, WH (1940) *The Varieties of Human Physique*. New York: Harper & Row.

Tanner, JM (1970) in PH Mussen (ed) *Carmichaels' manual of Child Psychology*. (Vol.1) New York: Wiley.

Thomas, A and Chess, S (1977) *Temperament and Development*. New York: Brunner/Mazel.

Thomas, R M (1994) The meaning and significance of ethnicity in educational discourse. *International Review of Education*. 40(1): 74–80.

UNESCO (United Nations Educational, Scientific and Cultural Organisation) (1994) *The Salamanca Statement and Framework for Action on Special Needs Education*. Paris:UNESCO.

Vygotsky, LS (1962) *Thought and Language*. New York: Wiley.

Walker, RN (1962) 'Body build and behaviour in young children: 1. Body and nursery school teachers' ratings', *Monograph of the Society for Research in Child Development*, 27 (Whole No. 84).

Warnock Report (1978) *Special Educational Needs: Report of the Committee of Enquiry into the Education of Handicapped Children and Young People*. London: HMSO.

Williams, JR and Scott, RB (1953) 'Growth and development of Negro infants: IV. Motor development and its relationships to child rearing practices in two groups of Negro infants', *Child Development*, 24: 103–21.

Witkin, HA, Dyk, RB, Faterson, HF, Goodenough, DR and Karp, SA (1962) *Psychological Differentiation*. New York: Wiley.

Wragg, EC (1994) *Managing Behaviour*, BBC Video and Book. London: BBC Education.

Yarrow LJ, Rubenstein, JL, Pedersen, FA and Jankowski, JJ (1972) 'Dimensions of early stimulation and their differential effects on infant development', *Merrill-Palmer Quarterly*, 18: 205–18.

Chapter 3

Badger, B (1992) 'Changing a disruptive school', in D Reynolds and P Cuttance (eds) *School Effectiveness: Research, Policy and Practice*. London: Cassell.

Bandler, R and Grinder, J (1975) *The Structure of Magic 1*. Paulo Alto, CA: Science and Behaviour Books.

Blank, M (1985) *Instructional and Classroom Discourse*. Boston, MA: The Language Learning Disabilities Institute, Emerson College.

Blank, M and Marquis, A (1987) *Teaching Discourse*. Tuscon, AZ: Communication Skill Builders.

Bloom, BS (1956) *Taxonomy of Educational Objectives: Cognitive Domain*. New York: David McKay.

Burleson, BR (1984) 'Comforting communication', in H Sypher and J Applegate (eds) *Communication by Children and Adults*. Beverly Hills, CA:Sage.

Burleson, BR (1991) 'Comforting messages: their significance and effects', in JA Daly and JM Wiemann (eds) *Communicating Strategically: Strategies in Interpersonal Communication*. Hillsdale, NJ: Lawrence Erlbaum.

Crystal, D (1971) *Linguistics*. Harmondsworth: Penguin.

Delamont, S (1976) *Interaction in the Classroom*. London: Methuen.

Ekenrode, J (1984) 'Impact of chronic and acute stressors on daily reports of mood', *Journal of Personality and Social Psychology*, 46: 907–918.

Ekman, P, and Friesen, WV (1972) 'Hand movements', *Journal of Communication*, 22: 353–74.

Fenton, JV (1973) *Choice of Habit*. New York: Macdonald and Evans.

Fortenberry, JH, Maclean, J, Morris, P and O'Connell (1972) 'Mode of dress as a perceptual cue to deference', *Journal of Social Psychology*, 104: 131–9.

Gage, NL (1968) *Explorations of the Teacher's Effectiveness in Explaining*. Stanford, CA: Stanford University Press.

Mehrabin, A (1972) *Non-verbal Communication*. New York: Aldine Atherton.

Miller, L (1984) 'Problem solving hypothesis testing and language disorders', in GP Wallach and KG Butler (eds), *Language Learning Disabilities in School-age Children*. Baltimore, MD: Williams & Wilkins.

Pate, RT and Bremer, NH (1967) 'Guiding learning through skilful questioning', *The Elementary School Journal*, 67: 417–22.

Perls, FS (1969) *Gestalt Therapy Verbatim*. Utah: Moab, Real People Press.

Sage, R (2000a) *The Communication Opportunity Group*. Leicester: The University of Leicester Press.

Sage, R (2000b) *Class Talk*. Stafford: Network Educational Press.

Sage, R (2003) *Lend Us Your Ears*. Stafford: Network Educational Press.

Smith, A (1998) *Accelerated Learning in Practice*. Stafford: Network Educational Press.

Susskind, K (1979) 'Encouraging teachers to encourage children's curiosity', in *Journal of Clinical Child Psychology*, 8: 101–6.

Taba, H (1966) *Teaching Strategies and Cognitive Functioning in Elementary Schools*, USIOE Co-operative Research Project No. 1574, San Francisco, CA: San Francisco State College.

Wheldell, K, Bevan, K and Shortall, K (1986) 'A touch of reinforcement: the effects of contingent teacher touch on the classroom behaviour of young children', *Educational Review*, 38 (3): 207–16.

Wragg, EC (1993) *Class Management*. London: Methuen.

Wragg, EC (1994) *Managing Behaviour*, BBC Video and Book. London: BBC Education.

Chapter 4

Bartlett, S, Burton, D, Peim, N (2001) *Introduction to Education Studies*. London: Paul Chapman Publishing.

Bennathan, M and Boxall, M (1996) *Effective Intervention in Primary Schools: Nurture Groups*. London: Fulton.

Boxall, M (2000) 'The nuture group in the primary school', in M. Bennathan and M. Boxall (eds.) *Effective Intervention in Primary Schools: Nurture Groups*, London: David Fulton.

Cajkler, W (1999) 'Misconceptions in the NLS: National Literacy Strategy or no linguistic sense?' *Use of English*, 50(3): 214–27.

Cajkler, W (2002) 'Literacy across the curriculum at KS3: more muddle and confusion', *Use of English*, 53(2): 151–64.

Cajkler, W and Hislam, J (2002) 'The butler was dead is not a passive form: how grammar has been misconceived and misapplied in the National Curriculum', proceedings of the British Educational Research Association, p 34. University of Exeter, September.

Carr, W and Hartnett (1996) *Education and the Struggle for Democracy: The Politics of Educational Ideas.* Buckingham: Open University Press.

Cooper, P (2001) *We Can Work it out – a Review of What Works with SEBD.* Ilford: Barnados.

Cohen, L et al (2000) *Research Methods in Education.* London: Routledge.

Davis, K and Moore, WE (1967) 'Some principles of stratification', in R Bendix and SM Lipset (eds) *Class, Status and Power.* London: Kegan Paul.

Dearing, R (1994) *The Final Report: National Curriculum and its Assessment.* SCAA.

Department of Education and Science (DES) (1989) *The Task Group on Assessment and Testing: a Report.* London: HMSO.

DfEE (1998) *The National Literacy Strategy: Framework for Teaching.* London: DfEE.

DfEE (1999) *The National Numeracy Strategy: Framework for Teaching Mathematics.* London: DfEE.

DfEE (1999a) *The National Curriculum: Handbook for Primary Teachers in England, Key Stages 1 and 2.* London: DfEE, www.nc.uk.net.

DfEE (2000) *Teaching Assistant File: Induction Training for Teaching Assistants* London: DfEE.

DfEE (2000a) *Working with Teaching Assistants: A Good Practice Guide.* London: DfEE.

DfES (2002) a–z www.dfes.gov.uk August 2002.

DfES (2004) *Five Year Strategy for Children and Learners.* London: HMSO www.dfes.gov.uk/publications/5yearstrategy.

Gill, D and Adams, B (1989) *ABC of Communication Studies.* London: Macmillan Education.

Gipps, C and Stobart, G (1993) *Assessment.* London: Hodder & Stoughton.

Green, S (2000) *Research Methods in Health, Social and Early Years Care.* Cheltenham: Stanley Thornes.

Hancock and Mansfield (2001) 'The Literacy Hour: a case for listening to children' in J Collins, K Insley and J Soler (eds) *Developing Pedagogy, Researching Practice.* Buckingham: Open University Press.

Hargreaves, D (1994) 'Coherence and manageablity', in A Pollard and J Bourne, *Teaching and Learning in the Primary School.* London: Routledge.

Hedderwick, M (1986) *Katie Morag Delivers the Mail.* London: HarperCollins.

Hughes, P (2000) *Principles of Primary Education Study Guide.* London: Fulton.

HMI 434, (2002) *Teaching Assistants in Primary Schools: An Evaluation of the Quality and Impact of their Work.* London: HMSO.

Lawton, D (1999) *Beyond the National Curriculum.* London: Hodder & Stoughton.

Lees, J, Smithies, G, and Chambers, C (2001) 'Let's talk: a community–based language promotion project for sure start', in proceedings of the RCSLT National Conference: Sharing Communication, Birmingham, April.

Mann, JF (1979) *Education*. London: Pitman.

Moseley, J (1996) *Quality Circle Time*. London: Fulton.

National Curriculum Online www.nc.uk.net.

Norwood Report (1943) Board of Education, *Curriculum and Examinations in Secondary Schools*. London: HMSO.

Office for Standards in Education (OFSTED) (2000) *The Annual Report of Her Majesty's Chief Inspector of Schools. Standard and Quality in Education 1988/99*. London: HMSO.

The Qualifications and Curriculum Authority (QCA) www.qca.org.uk.

QCA (2000) *Could Try Harder – The LEARN Project: Guidance for Schools on Assessment for Learning*. London: HMSO.

QCA (2002a) *Designing and Timetabling the Primary Curriculum*. London: HMSO.

QCA (2002b) *School Sampling Project*. London: HMSO.

Ross, A (2001) 'What is the curriculum? in J Collins, K Insley and J Soler (eds) *Developing Pedagogy, Researching Practice*. Buckingham: Open University Press.

Ryan, A (1994) 'Preserving integration within the national curriculum in primary schools', in A Pollard and J Bourne, *Teaching and Learning in the Primary School*. London: Routledge.

Sage, R (2000a) *The Communication Opportunity Group*. Leicester: The University of Leicester.

Sage, R (2000b) *Class Talk*. Stafford: Network Educational Press.

Trowler, P (1995) *Investigating Education and Training*. London: Collins Educational.

Watkinson, A (2002) *Assisting Learning and Supporting Teaching*. London: Fulton.

Young, MFD (1998) *The Curriculum of the Future: From the New Sociology of Education to a Critical Theory of Learning*. London: Falmer Press.

Woodhead, C (1999) Department for Education and Employment (DfEE) Report of the Chief Inspector of Schools. London: DfEE.

Chapter 5

Abbott, J (1994) *Learning Makes Sense: Recreating Education for a Changing Future*. Letchworth: Education 2000.

Bruce, T and Meggitt, C (2000) *Child Care and Education* (2nd edn). London:Hodder and Stoughton.

DfEE (2001) *Delivering Results: A Strategy to 2006*. London: HMSO.

DfES (1990) *Starting with Quality: report of the committee of inquiry into the quality of educational experience offered to three and four year olds* (Rumbold report). London: HMSO.

Gardener, H (1984) www.acceleratedlearning.com/

Green, S (2000) *Research Methods in Health, Social and Early Years Care*. Cheltenham: Nelson Thornes.

HMI 434 (2002) *Teaching Assistants in Primary Schools: An Evaluation of the Quality and Impact of their Work*. London: HMSO.

Lloyd, S (1992) *The Phonics Handbook*. Chigwell: Jolly Learning.

McCarthy, B (2002) www.4mat.com

Montgomery, D (2002) *Helping Teachers Develop Through Classroom Observation*. London: David Fulton.

Nortledge, A (1990) *The Good Study Guide*. Buckingham: Open University Press.

Sage, R (2003) *Lend Us Your Ears: Listen and Learn*. Stafford: Network Educational Press.

Thompson, B and Calder, P (1998) 'Early years educators: skills, knowledge and understanding', in L Abbott and G Pugh (eds) *Training to Work in the Early Years*. Buckingham: Open University Press.

Index